IRISH SYMBOLS OF 3500 BC

IRISH
SYMBOLS
OF 3500 BC

by

N. L. Thomas

MERCIER PRESS

MERCIER PRESS
PO Box 5, 5 French Church Street, Cork
16 Hume Street, Dublin 2

© N. L. Thomas, 1988

A CIP record is available for this book from the British Library.

ISBN 0 85342 856 5

10 9 8 7 6 5 4 3

Printed in Ireland by Colour Books Ltd.

Contents

List of illustrations and plates 6

Map of Ireland 8

Preface 9

1. **The Beginning** 11
   *Man's early development, the Middle East compared
   with north-west Europe, Newgrange and Knowth*

2. **The Symbols** 25
   *Language and ancient scripts, Irish symbols,
   other civilisations*

3. **The Calendar** 32
   *Locations of Knowth, Mount Pleasant, the
   Sanctuary, Woodhenge and Stonehenge descriptions*

4. **Stone Inscriptions** 49
   Newgrange, Knowth, Loughcrew, Fourknocks

5. **Legend and Myth** 79
   *The Irish invasions, Thirty-three, the deities,
   pre-history, Christianity, an Irish chronology,
   the Norse story of the creation*

Appendix 1: Dates and dating 92
Appendix 2: The Mount Pleasant calendar 95

Acknowledgements 104
Bibliography 105
Index 107

List of Illustrations and Plates

Map of Ireland	*page* 8
The Mound at Newgrange *(plate)*	17
View of Interior of Knowth Mound *(plate)*	19
Irish Symbols (fourth millennium BC)	29, 30
Numerical Symbols of Various Civilisations	31
Locations of Calendar Buildings	33
Plan of Knowth Passage Mound	36
Knowth Kerb Stone, K 13	38
Knowth Kerb Stone, K 13 *(plate)*	39
Knowth Kerb Stone, K 14	41
Knowth Kerb Stone, K 15 *(plate)*	42
Knowth Calendar	43
Knowth Kerb Stone, K 15	44
The Newgrange Entrance Stone, K 1	50
Newgrange Kerb Stone, K 52	53
Newgrange Kerb Stone, K 52 *(plate)*	53
Newgrange Roof Stone, East Chamber	54
Knowth Kerb Stone, K 11	56
Knowth Kerb Stone, K 74	57
Knowth Kerb Stone, K 74 *(plate)*	57
Knowth Kerb Stone, K 36	59
Knowth Kerb Stone, K 36 *(plate)*	59
Knowth Kerb Stone, K 38	60
Knowth Kerb Stone, K 43	60
Knowth Kerb Stone, K 53	62
Knowth Kerb Stone, K 53 *(plate)*	62
Knowth Kerb Stone, K 65	63
Knowth Kerb Stone, K 65 *(plate)*	63
Knowth Kerb Stone, K 78	65
Knowth Kerb Stone, K 78 *(plate)*	65

Knowth Kerb Stone, K 79   67
Knowth Kerb Stone, K 79 *(plate)*   67
Knowth Kerb Stone, K 81   69
Knowth Kerb Stone, K 81 *(plate)*   69
Loughcrew, The Calendar Stone   72
Loughcrew, Cairn F, Stone C 1   73
Loughcrew, Slieve na Calliagh *(plate)*   74
Fourknocks Passage   75
Solitaire Board   77
Mount Pleasant Calendar   96
Calendar Events Comparison   101

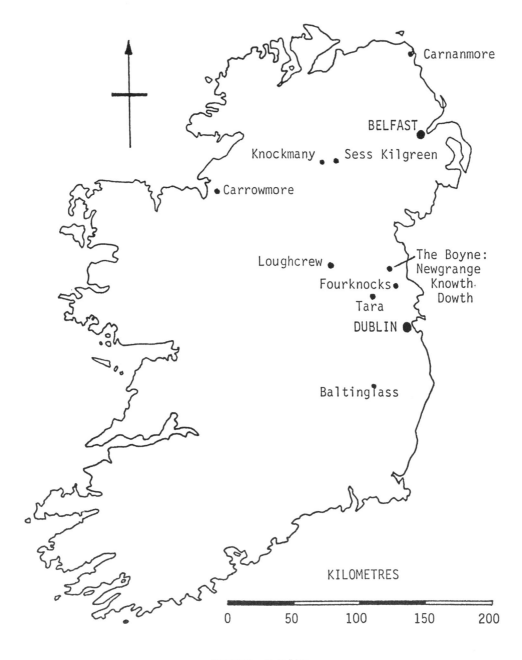

Carnanmore

BELFAST

Knockmany • • Sess Kilgreen

• Carrowmore

Loughcrew • The Boyne:
Newgrange
Fourknocks • Knowth
Dowth
Tara •

DUBLIN •

Baltinglass •

KILOMETRES

0   50   100   150   200

IRELAND

Preface

It was a series of coincidences that led me to the problem posed by the fourth millennium inscriptions on the stones comprising the ancient Irish mounds of Newgrange and Knowth and the associated monuments.

Many students have previously studied and described the inscriptions and their monographs talk in terms of artistry and ornamentation. Whilst it is clearly valid to discuss the inscriptions in these terms, I formed the tentative opinion that the ancient Irish people were trying to convey a message in their artwork. This was a difficult problem to solve. Let me attempt to answer the question by a parallel example.

Two hundred and fifty kilometres west of Alice Springs in central Australia is a small aboriginal settlement. Their activities include the making of painted canvases in a unique style. Each painting is composed of hundreds of acrylic paint dots made with a stick dipped in the paint, placed very carefully on the canvas. The patterns represent stylistic aboriginal motifs. Various shades of the basic colours are used; black, white, red, brown, yellow — the colours of the Australian bush. The designs include concentric circles, dots, hoops, lines and snake patterns.

The completed paintings are most striking and artistically attractive. It is when the viewer appreciates the fundamentals of each artistic creation that a fuller understanding is attained.

For instance, one particularly attractively designed and important canvas is actually a geographical map of an area many hundreds of square kilometres in extent; each painted design element represented on the canvas is a waterhole, a track, a gorge, a food area, in fact all the essential qualities for successful living in the dry centre of the continent. Other canvases tell of the mythological dreamtime, the trials and tribulations of the traveller, stories concerning their ancestors.

Five thousand years ago in Ireland, the people of those days created what are now the oldest buildings in Europe. Their artistic ornamentation on the stones of which the structures were built also has a message to tell in symbolic terms of their sixteen month calendar. My intrepretation of a reasonable proportion of the inscriptions are variations on this basic theme. It may well be that other inscriptions can be deciphered to tell the tales of the myths and deities. It is hoped this may prove to be the case. In the meantime the reader is invited to consider the evidence presented, the related factual matters, the myths recounted and the deductions made.

Neil L. Thomas
Melbourne, 1987

CHAPTER ONE

THE BEGINNING

If you miss the first buttonhole, you will
not succeed in buttoning up your coat.
                              Goethe 1749-1832

At the peak of the last ice age about 25,000 years ago, Ireland, Britain and north-western Europe were largely covered with ice and snow. The glaciers began to recede and a gradual rise in global temperatures occurred and by the tenth millennium BC the warmer climate made it possible for the land to support the few hundred people who hunted for their livelihood. The further improvement in the next few thousand years enabled the land to support small bands of nomads who hunted prey and fished in the rivers and oceans for their living. By the sixth millennium, the population of about 5,000 persons was living in the 335,000 square kilometres, the land feeding one or two persons per hundred square kilometres. An estimated 10,000 persons would have lived there in 5000 BC although the climate was colder than it is today. The small scattered mesolithic population was mostly occupied in the search for food, having little time for the creation of stone monuments to be discovered by today's archaeologists. The continental circumstances were very similar in the north and west.

It is well to provide a perspective to these happenings by recounting the principal events in the Biblical

communities in the warmer Middle Eastern lands where the archaeology and history are comparatively well known. In the more southerly latitudes, the warmer climate and less rigorous conditions made possible man's great leap forward from nomadic hunter to urban dweller about 10,000 BC. At Jericho, a short distance north of the Dead Sea in the valley of the Jordan river, a copious flow of fresh water from a spring made it possible for a permanent settlement to become established at the oasis in the middle of an otherwise barren valley. The settlement was the oldest walled city yet known, the massive surrounding wall and look-out tower ten metres or so in height demonstrating a remarkable degree of social order, public works and organisation. The estimated population of about a thousand or more was supported by agriculture based on the waters of the spring and the irrigation of crops. Several harvests would have been possible each year.

Three thousand years later, about 7000 BC, a settlement of five to six thousand people lived at a place named Catal Huyuk in what is now southern Turkey. The archaeological record shows the first pottery, the first textiles, the first mirrors, wooden vessels and wall paintings. The inhabitants clearly had an organised society, an agriculture based on irrigation and they engaged in trade and commerce. By the end of the first period of settlement about 6000 BC, attempts at pottery decoration were evident.

Taking another leap forward of three thousand years, we find the Sumerian city of Uruk was established by 3000 BC near the confluence of the Tigris and Euphrates rivers. It is there that the first evidence was found of writing on small clay tablets incised with simplified pictographic signs to represent objects. They are also attributed with the invention of the wheel.

In all these Middle Eastern countries, their designs of houses, streets and cities, their granaries, temples and ziggurats were essentially rectangular. There were only a few circular structures such as towers and wells. We have evidence of the writing, linear measurement units and their arithmetical ability to account for granary stocks and commercial transactions.

There were, however, essential differences between these southern communities and those of the north and west; principally the colder and wetter northern climate, the more sparsely distributed population, forests of timber in place of clay for building materials. At northern latitudes there would have been greater awareness of the sun's and moon's characteristic behaviour because of the more marked differences between summer and winter, the longer days of summer and the shorter days in the cold months. The further one is away from the equator, the longer are the periods of dawn and dusk. The magnified size of the sun's and moon's orb at those times of the day greatly enhances an observer's awareness. Particularly in the case of the moon, it is possible to see the dark and light patterns of the lunar landscape, enlarged by the refraction of the atmosphere.

By 4000 BC, the improved northern climate and the advent of agriculture together with population increases enabled the newly skilled northern peoples to settle more or less permanently on suitable uplands where they felled the trees and created pasture for their

cattle and arable land for their crops. With these
changes and more leisure time resulting from a settled
life came the ability to see distant horizons unobscured
by the forests. With this awareness and the time to
study the behaviour of the celestial bodies would have
come the accumulation of knowledge which led to
megalithic monuments' construction and the circular
timber buildings we know of today. About this time,
the neolithic communities began the great works such
as Stonehenge and the many other megalithic monuments still to be seen over northern and western
Europe. An estimated 20,000 people lived in the Irish
and British islands by this time and proportionate numbers in north-west Europe. They clearly had the collec-
tive abilities and organisation, the motivation and the
skills to construct hundreds of stone circles in the
northern and western parts of the country, to build
Silbury Hill, the largest prehistoric man made mound
in Europe, the many henges, earthworks and barrows
in Ireland and Britain. Two thousand years later the
population would have reached about 50,000 and probably around 100,000 by 1000 BC.

These favourable conditions degenerated during the
first millennium BC due to lower temperatures and
more rainfall, factors which may account for the lesser
numbers of ancient monuments of a notable kind such
as Stonehenge. There were however a great many hill
forts built in this millennium indicating activity of a
different kind.

By the time of the Roman invasion which commenced
in 54 BC, the population numbered about half a million.
The stability and prosperity of Roman Britain allowed

further expansion and with it came the imposition of Roman law and customs, language and measurements. In Britain, the southern part of the country was colonised but in the north and west the Roman rule was much more tenuous and the old prehistoric customs and religious beliefs continued to be followed, albeit less organised and widespread than in previous ages. After the collapse of the Roman Empire and the withdrawal of the Romans from Britain about AD 485, conditions began to deteriorate. Later, the invasion of what is now England by the Saxons caused much hardship and the population fell from two and a half million to one and a half million during the century from AD 500 to AD 600. Those times have become known as the Dark Ages. Parallel events in Europe had similar effects. The impact of these events since the birth of Christ undoubtedly affected the quality and volume of prehistoric knowledge handed on from generation to generation in what had become Celtic society.

The old religions and beliefs, the social customs and society generally continued with little alteration in Scandinavia. In Ireland and to a degree in Scotland, Wales and the west of England, folklore and customs were handed on from one generation to the next around the crofters' fireside by the telling of tales, reciting sagas of adventure, of kings and battles. Within recent memory, the Celtic method of learning was practised in the Scottish Western Isles. Each Sunday, the children of the area were gathered together and learned to recite their family tree back for twenty generations or more. Not for them the dependancy on the written word, the accent was on training children's memories.

This was probably the way knowledge was passed on in neolithic times when Stonehenge was built, in the bronze ages of the second millennium, in the iron age before the Romans and their Empire. We know of Celtic folklore stories which were not written down until AD 1300 and which can be dated from Roman historical records. They were handed on from bard to bard for hundreds of years with little if any alteration. The absence of baked clay tablets, of papyrus scrolls and other records like those of Sumeria and Egypt, of Greece and Rome should not lead the man of today to the conclusion they had any lesser knowledge or abilities, only that it is a little harder to recreate a picture of their life and times. Human abilities can hardly have changed in the last two hundred generations. Apart from superficial appearances, people thought, acted and looked basically as they do today. Our forefathers' limitations resulted from the lesser quantity of information bequeathed to successive generations and their skills in making use of that knowledge.

This book has the objective of showing that the inhabitants of Ireland in the fourth millennium BC had a well developed philosophy concerning the creation of the world, a calendar and an assembly of symbols each with a specific meaning.

The Newgrange passage mound is the second oldest building in Europe; older than the vast majority of Middle Eastern ancient monuments, it is preceded only by the round tower at Jericho, Israel, and the decayed remains at Catal Huyuk, Turkey. Between 1962 and 1975, the Irish authorities proceeded to carefully restore Newgrange to a condition as close as possible to the

The Mound at Newgrange

original. The visitor today views the imposing facade of quartz stone, the entrance portal and doorway and the roof box over the lintel which admits midwinter's day dawn rays of the rising sun. A truly commendable restoration project.

Complementing Newgrange are two other passage mounds, Knowth and Dowth. The three are the principal ancient monuments within the sweeping bend of the river Boyne and it is well to provide a brief account of these evidences of megalithic art and skills.

The Knowth mound is north-west of Newgrange, directly aligned on a minor lunar standstill, north 56 degrees west, and at a distance of 1.3 kilometres. The complementary Dowth mound is also on a minor lunar standstill alignment, this time north 59 degrees east, and at a distance of two kilometres. Both mounds have passages with solar alignments. At Knowth, the two passages into the mound are aligned with sunrise and sunset at the equinox. A short passage into the Dowth mound is aligned with the midwinter sunset at solstice, complementing the sunrise passage on the same day at Newgrange. A second longer passage, the entrance to which was blocked during recent works, is thought to have an alignment of the calendrical quarter days in November and February.

When considered in relation to Newgrange, a number of other standing stones and earthworks within the bend of the river provided a series of solar and lunar alignments, the totality of which shows the area was constructed according to a precise astronomical plan. The full design would have provided a form of calendar for the neolithic inhabitants, and the three passage

View of Interior of Knowth Mound

mounds the magic dwelling places for their deities. The entire area was presumably held in very high regard as a sacred site by the population.

The construction of the three passage mounds and the planning of the site commenced well over five millennia ago. Two significant radio carbon dates derived from samples obtained in the roof of the passage into Newgrange were 2475 ± 45 years bc (Grn — 5462) and 2465 ± 40 years bc (Grn — 5463), both indicating a building period about 3200 BC in corrected terms. The nearby Knowth mound excavations have produced radio carbon samples at the lower levels dated at 2795 ± 165 years bc (UB — 357), 2845 ± 185 years bc (UB — 319) and 2925 ± 160 years bc (UB — 318); from which it would be reasonable to infer a construction date of about 3500 BC, perhaps a century either way. Such dating makes Knowth passage mound quite clearly the oldest building in Europe. The great antiquity of the area can be fully appreciated.

I have reported in *Stonehenge Sunsets and Thirty-Three,* that the four British ancient monuments of the middle third millennium BC have been examined and these circular timber and stone buildings in southern England all had a full count of 365 days, a sixteen month year divided into sixty-four weeks, each of five days. Intercalary days were added to each four week cycle to complete the month, two or three days as required.

Mount Pleasant henge and calendar building was built about 2600 BC no doubt reflecting the conviction of the hierarchy and the general population of its worth. The community effort needed to construct a building of forty metres diameter with timber posts was clearly considerable and it would have required the co-operation of the prehistoric inhabitants over an extensive area. It has been estimated the selection and felling of the required quantity of oak trees of sufficient maturity would have encompassed an area many kilometres in diameter. Only sketchy information indicates the population numbers in the area, but clearly the results of their efforts shows the substantially metropolitan nature of the central portion of southern England. Other major neolithic centres were Maumbury Rings about 1½ kilometres away and Maiden Castle at a distance of 4½ kilometres.

The Sanctuary calendar building on the hill near West Overton, Wiltshire, has been stated to have been contemporary with Avebury and was probably constructed before 2500 BC. Its design embraces both solar and lunar calendars.

At Woodhenge, near Stonehenge, Wiltshire, concrete markers now indicate another calendar building from about 2500 BC. The structure was egg shaped in plan and the presumed design is more complex than the two earlier examples which comprised concentric circles of posts and stones.

At the beginning of the second millennium, Stonehenge apparently replaced Woodhenge as the principal calendar building and is believed to have continued in use well into the first millennium BC.

It is interesting to note that Mount Pleasant and Woodhenge were clearly 365 day solar calendars with no inexplicable features that can be linked with the behaviour of the moon. In the case of Stonehenge, however, it is believed it commenced as a purely lunar calendar and later became a joint solar/lunar calendar, outlasting its predecessors by one thousand five hundred years and more.

I have recently perceived a relationship between the Boyne valley mounds and these four British monuments.

The Knowth kerb stone K 15 is inscribed with a fan shaped design of sixteen radiating lines. Originating at a common point, each ray ends at a rectangle incised on the stone. Other symbols on the stone are thought to relate to the number of days in a month. The design is discussed in detail in chapter two.

Another element of the design is the semi-circular twin arc lines which enclose an inner area. Clearly a significant part of the stone inscription, a link is seen with the description of the firmament as the sky above the earth. The Norse myth of the creation of the world is recounted in chapter five, page 79. The reader will appreciate the similarity between the twin semi-circular arc lines and the inverted bowl placed above the man's earth which formed the firmament.

By way of confirmation of the Knowth kerb stone design, I examined a contemporary design incised on a stone at Loughcrew, forty kilometres west of Knowth. The Gaelic name of the hilltop site is Slieve na Calliagh, the hills of the witch. This may have derived from the ancient reverence with which a sacred site would have been held. With the coming of Christianity the Church would have given a name to the area designed to discourage the ancient beliefs, hence the appellation.

This design too has the same elements, the sixteen ray fan design and twin arc lines surrounding an inner area with a central mark. The pattern is illustrated on page 72.

That two sites should portray the same basic concept indicates an established set of ideas on the part of those ancient peoples. What those beliefs were is a difficult question to solve.

I have attempted to explain the Irish symbols of 3500 BC in terms of the four British calendar buildings linked with the mythology of the north-western European peoples.

Irish mythology accounts for the settlement of ancient Ireland in terms of six invasions by successive waves of peoples who settled the Isle of Erin. The first invaders settled in a land that already existed in very ancient times. They were followed at intervals by other peoples whom the myth links with deities and the conquests.

It is curious that Irish mythology has no recorded account of the myth of the creation of their world. A fundamental myth of this kind is a central theme in all ancient civilisations' beliefs. Early man clearly felt the need to explain the creation of their world in terms that could be understood and accepted by the general population.

I have resorted to the Norse myth of the creation of the world in an attempt to explain the twin arc lines above the sixteen ray fan element of the two designs. For completeness, the entire Norse myth is retold in chapter five, abridged slightly to reveal the essential matters uncluttered by conversational embellishments contained in the original translation from the Icelandic. In the myth, the part that describes how the sky was formed is most pertinent. It was created when Odin took the skull of the dead frost giant Ymir and placed it over man's domain as a form of protection from the other frost giants. By creating the firmament in this way, and placing the stars in their positions and the clouds in the sky, an understandable story was made in terms of man and woman's day to day experiences.

The twin arc lines are supposed to represent the idea of a section cutting the skull to show its curved form extending down to man's earth on all sides. The rays are considered to be the concept of the sun rising at dawn on each of the first days of the sixteen months in a year.

The other symbols are interpreted in the manner described.

CHAPTER TWO

The Symbols

There is an art of reading, as well as an
art of thinking, and an art of writing.
                    Isaac D'Israeli 1766-1848

In any society there are those whose abilities place them well above the majority of the community by virtue of their achievements and the respect in which they are held by the many. Researchers skilled in their fields have written about prehistoric society, its activities and the classes of people. In general terms, the 'priestly' class is believed to have been the repository of knowledge and their abilities enabled them to become the rulers of their society. Building was the responsibility of artisans; farmers formed the majority of the population and produced the food needed by the community. This was the basic structure of society the world over.

The educated and literate 'priests' amongst the early civilisations were clearly in the minority and it is to them we are indebted for the record of their life and times. Because of the several thousands of years that have elapsed between the early civilisations and our age today, it is true to say without any need for emphasis that virtually all the written records we are aware of were preserved in clay tablets and by inscriptions on stone.

History is defined as the written record of events; in

very general terms it began about 5000 years ago as the clay tablets of Sumeria testify. The importance of the Irish inscriptions will be appreciated when a comparison is made. Quite evidently the interpretation placed on the passage mound symbols shows a culture already firmly established by 3500 BC. It was clearly in possession of a philosophy and a calendar which presumably had taken many generations to develop.

The written history of the north-western peoples of Europe is presently accepted as beginning in the first millennium BC: the import of the conclusions reached in this book indicates the need to revise the idea; the threshold should be moved back in time to a date comparable with Sumeria. Admittedly not in the quantity of work but certainly in the standard of ideas. No longer should the millennia BC be termed pre-history.

Nowadays we learn to read by learning the alphabet letters and then how to use these symbols in groups to form words, and then the sequence of words to form sentences that tell the written story. In ancient Ireland, their symbols were apparently used to tell of two basic matters. The first was the sixteen month calendar and the second the idea of the world we live in, explained in terms of the sun, the moon, the imagined Other-world outside and beyond our immediate perception.

The interpretations I have placed on the thirty or more Irish symbols are stated on the following pages; the symbols – the meaning and a form of explanation or an example is given for each. Then in chapter three 'The Calendar' the incised designs on the various kerb stones and lintels are analysed, and by applying the presumed meaning of each symbol, the interpretation and meaning of a full design is described.

Other Lands and Other Tongues

The philologists responsible for deciphering and interpreting the ancient Middle Eastern scripts have mostly had the benefit of dual language inscriptions; the famous Rosetta stone from Egypt for example, was inscribed in two languages – ancient Egyptian and Greek. The French scholar Champollian deciphered the Egyptian hieroglyphs by comparing them with the Greek text which he could read directly. He also realised the Coptic language still used in the native Christian church in Egypt was a direct descendant of the ancient Egyptian tongue. He was thus able to interpret the Rosetta stone text and open the door to a study of the multitude of ancient Egyptian inscriptions. Similar success stories can be told of other tongues.

The Celts who migrated from Europe to Ireland and Britain towards the end of the first millennium BC used the Latin alphabet and numerical symbols in expressing wholly Celtic matters. Scholars were greatly aided in their understanding of the language by this, it being only necessary to have a working knowledge of the Roman tongue.

The pre-Celtic inhabitants of Ireland have offered no such dual language inscriptions for today's students. Without some key of that kind into the meaning of the ancient Irish inscriptions, interpretation is very difficult. The limited success achieved so far has stemmed directly from my study of the third millennium BC British calendar buildings, extended to the fourth millennium BC Irish passage mounds of Newgrange,

Knowth and Dowth.

In straightforward terms, script and writing can be divided into two kinds; pictograms, where a single symbol represents an object; alphabets, where group of symbols forms a word which represent an object. The Irish symbols are in the former category. An example of the latter is the Sumerian cruciform writing of c. 3500 BC. It is the earliest known system of writing, records having been discovered six kilometres north-east of Ur in Mesopotamia, now Iraq.

According to C. H. Gordon, the earliest known European texts are three unintelligible clay tablets from Tartaria, in Rumanian Transylvania, dated about the beginning of the third millennium BC. They are proof of early literacy in the Balkans and suggest connections with Sumeria. Beyond this it is hard to evaluate them historically and they cannot compare with the Minoan inscriptions of about 2000 BC, the first important language written in Europe.

A limited selection of symbols and definitions used by early civilisations affords a means of comparison with the Irish symbols; some marks are similar but in general it can be said the Irish symbols are mostly quite unique and it is considered they were developed independently. It may not be asserted a transfer of culture took place, for example that the Irish 'priests' of the fourth millennium BC learnt from the scribes of Uruk and Luxor. Particular symbols which have a degree of similarity are thought to be those where a truly basic characteristic determines the mark.

IRISH SYMBOLS, FOURTH MILLENNIUM BC
(See examples in chapters 3 and 4)

Definition	Symbol	Comment
A count of one	I ∧ ▲	one, alternative symbols
A set of units counted as one	∩	one month consists of four weeks
A count of five items, for example; instances are given from three to twenty-two and thirty-three	∿∿ ∿∿	each change of direction is counted as one K 13, K 36, K 38, K 53
A long line parallel to a row of other symbols indicates a whole consists of many parts	——————	sixteen months comprise one calendar year, K 13
Begin	๑	an instruction, K 13
End	๏	an instruction
A single day	o	K 15, K 43
Two days	◎	Sunday, Moonday?
Three days	◎	Wodensday, Thorsday, Freyrday? K 65
A group of days	๏	
An entity; a whole night and day, a week, a month, a quarter	◇	K 13, K 36
Half of a whole·	◈	K 13
Three diamond shapes meaning a count of three whole items, e.g.: three nights and days	◇◇◇	
Four weeks comprise one month	◈	K 13
Four quarters in a year, four seasons in a year	◈	K 13, K 36

IRISH SYMBOLS, FOURTH MILLENNIUM BC
(See examples in chapters 3 and 4)

Definition	*Symbol*	*Comment*
The firmament, the vault of the heavens		K 15, K 38, K 79, Loughcrew
The winter sun, a closely wound clockwise spiral		K 13, K15, K65, K79 The direction of rotation may sometimes change without any apparent change of meaning
The summer sun, a loosely wound anti-clockwise spiral		
The equinox, spring and autumn		The equinox days are of equal length, hence the dual spiral suns, K 13
A full moon		K 53
A new moon		K 53
Midday, noon, sky		K 65
Dawn and dusk		K 65
Start and finish of a statement		K 53 K38
Parallel lines indicating a route to be followed An alignment The stated direction		From days to weeks to months, to quarters, etc. K 13, K 36 See pages 50, 53, 57
A particular direction or bearing alignment		Mid-winter's day sunrise, page 54
A statement of eight or sixteen directions, the sense of every point of the compass		North, south, east, west and further halving of these basic directions

(The above K numbers refer to Knowth and Newgrange stones: chapters 3 and 4)

NUMERICAL SYMBOLS OF VARIOUS CIVILISATIONS

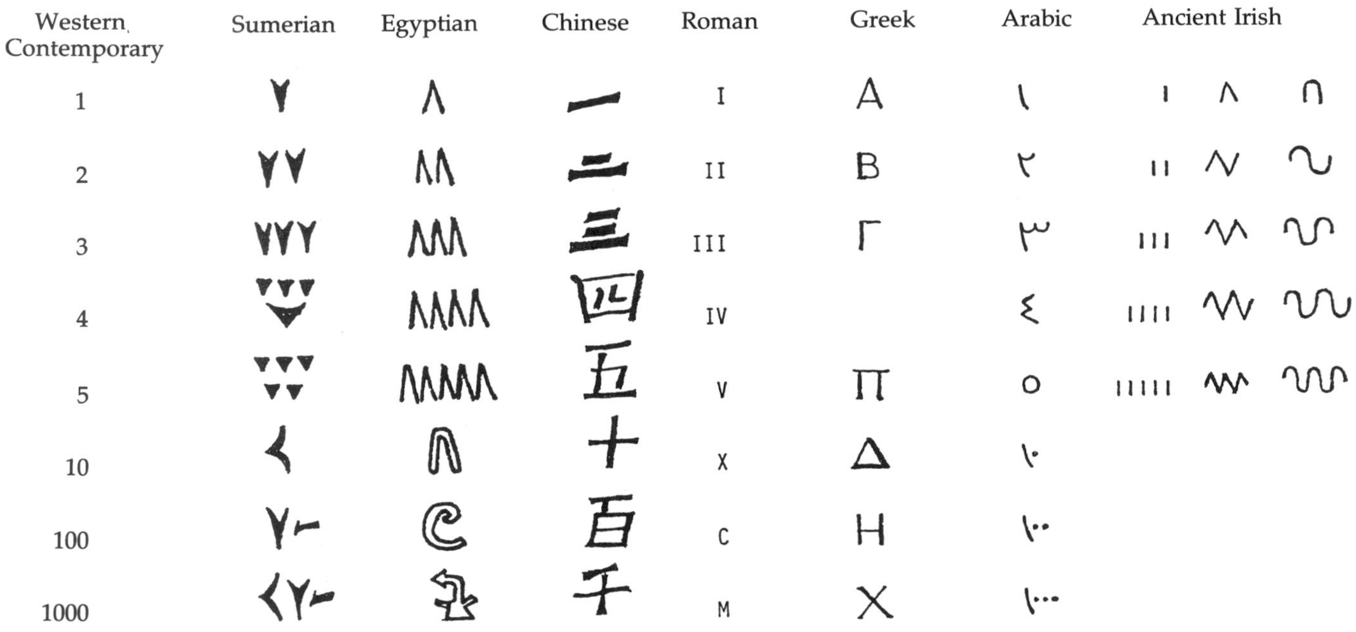

Western, Contemporary	Sumerian	Egyptian	Chinese	Roman	Greek	Arabic	Ancient Irish
1	𒁹	∧	一	I	Α	،	⌒ / ∧ / —
2	��	∧∧	二	II	Β	۲	∾ / ∧∧ / =
3		∧∧∧	三	III	Γ	۳	∾ / ∧∧∧ / ≡
4		∧∧∧∧	四	IV		۴	∿ / ∧∧∧∧ / ‖‖
5			五	V	Π	○	∿ / ∧∧∧∧∧ / ‖‖‖
10		∩	十	X	Δ	٠	
100		℮	百	C	Η	٠	
1000			千	M	Χ	٠	

CHAPTER THREE

THE CALENDAR

What is time? The shadow on the dial, the striking of the clock, the running of sand, day and night, summer and winter, months, years, centuries – these are but arbitrary and outward signs, the measure of time, not Time itself. Time is the Life of the soul.

Longfellow 1807-1882

The many laws of nature have complex results, the most noticeable of which are the number of days in a year and the changing pattern of those days. As a thinking and imaginative being, man has been continuing in his efforts to understand nature and to solve its vagaries. For early man the difficulty of devising an accurate calendar must have been considerable. The natural tendency to count in fives and tens is incompatible with the 365¼ days of the year, the four seasons and the changing duration of daylight between summer and winter; long summer days, then equal days and nights, the shorter winter days. The variable behaviour of the sun, and the moon's waxing and waning linked with the great complexity of its orbital behaviour, would have required considerable study and meticulous records for very many years to provide a basis for the creation of solar and lunar calendars.

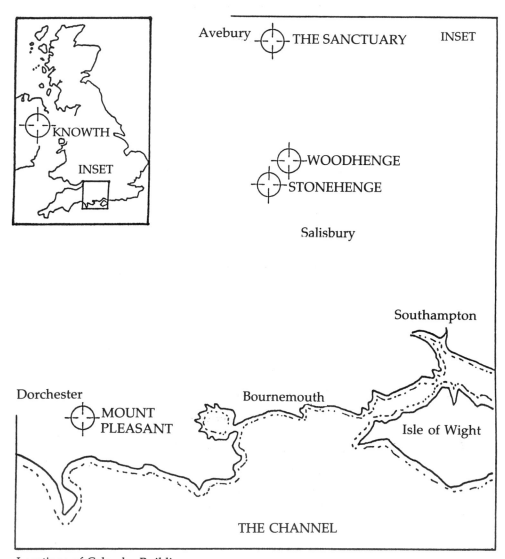

Locations of Calendar Buildings

Before 3500 BC, the native inhabitants of Ireland had apparently already solved these problems, as evidenced by the sixteen month solar calendar perceived from my study of markings on two large stones from the Knowth passage mound.

The calendar is the earliest known direct evidence of man's means of recording the progress of the natural year and of systematically measuring time.

Recent scientific archaeological excavations, land surveys, careful recording of the incised markings on over two hundred megaliths and an analysis of the artistry shown by the designs from the Newgrange, Knowth and Dowth passage mounds have all combined to reveal the most important group of fourth millennium BC monuments in Europe. The Knowth calendar serves to highlight the skills and abilities of those neolithic peoples. An analysis of the incised designs on the kerb stones K 13, K 14 and K 15 may be found difficult to assimilate at a first reading. In that case it is suggested the reader should return to a study of the Irish symbols portrayed on pages 29 and 30 in the previous chapter. A re-reading of the interpretations should help understanding.

The clear evidence of the considerable skill and logic required to design the calendar must have reflected a belief in the value of such activities which had the general support of the entire community. That conviction linked with the mathematical form of the calendar and the possible names of the elements points towards a formal philosophy and its widespread acceptance: in other words a religion based on solar and lunar calendars, symbolic numbers and a panoply of deities.

Experts have said there is no evidence that a sixteen month calendar was in fact in use at that time, even though the configuration of the designs is perceived. This specious assertion does not take into account the plain continuity of principle over many millennia, which give rise to the four later British building designs, all of which demonstrate the identical basic idea. For what other reason would the prehistoric men have designed and built such structures if not to demonstrate a live philosophy?

A reconstruction of the Irish calendar and the four British geometric designs and an analysis of the calendar portrayed at each of the sites has led to the working hypothesis the elements are seen to have consensus with the deities of folklore.

The sixteen months of the Irish calendar may have been named but no evidence has been found to enable any valid conclusions to be made. The best guess would appear to be the names of the four seasons and the four Celtic festivals for the odd numbered months; Summer, Autumn, Winter, Spring; and Lug, Samain, Imbolc and Beltane. The even numbered months are referred to by number: two, four, six, etc.

The idea of a five day week in 3500 BC is interesting; if any chosen day was a rest day, the names of each of the days, etc. Purely as an aid to understanding and as a reasonable working hypothesis it is suggested that the day names of the prehistoric five day week were the equivalent of the names we are familiar with. From the present, back through historical records of the Vikings' five day week, through the strong folklore traditions of the northern peoples and to the British monuments are

PLAN OF MOUND SHOWING
THE KERB STONES
AND EAST-WEST PASSAGES

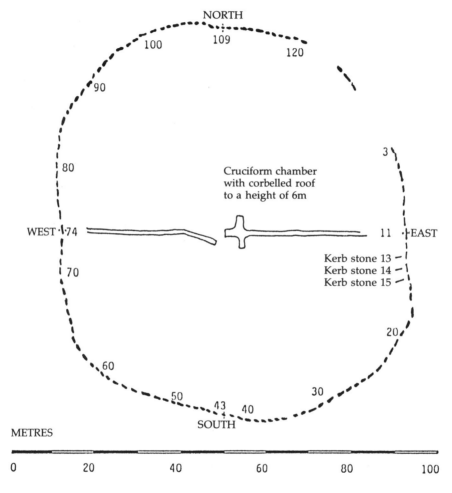

Plan of Knowth Passage Mound

many threads. Of our seven days, Tuesday and Satur-
day are names derived from pre-Christian Germanic
and Roman deities, Tiuw and Saturn. The other five
days are names for northern deities; Sunday is named
after the sun; Monday is the day of the moon; Wednes-
day is derived from Woden of British folklore, the same
deity as Odin of the Norse legends; Thursday is named
for the thunder god Thor; Freyr the god of fertility was
the origin of Friday. The names Sunday, Moonday,
Wodensday, Thorsday and Freyrday are used to clarify
the account and give colour to my texts *Stonehenge
Sunsets and Thirty-Three* and *British Neolithic Calendar
Buildings*.

   Critics may say there is no firm basis for suggesting
these names in discussions concerning prehistoric
calendar; whilst this is true in essence because no
written records exist, the adoption of the terms does
permit an understandable explanation. The four seasons
and the four quarterly festivals complement chosen
dates in the sixteen month year. As a working hypothesis it accounts for the archaeological findings at the
Irish and British sites, for the perceived elements in
myths and the folklore from Irish, Celtic, Welsh, Scottish and Norse sources.

Knowth, County Meath, Ireland c. 3500 BC

Knowth is the largest of three passage mounds within
the bend of the river Boyne, it is some ninety-five
metres in diameter and twelve metres high. Two
passages into the mound from the east and west are
aligned with the sunrise and sunset at the spring and
autumn equinox; their construction comprises vertical

stone slabs to the sides and horizontal lintels overhead. The western passage is about thirty-four metres in length and the eastern passage about forty metres. There are 127 kerb stones surrounding the mound, of these, three are particularly notable; they have been numbered K 13, K 14, K 15 by Professor George Eogan of the Department of Archaeology, University College, Dublin. The interpretations placed on the designs by me are as follows:

Kerb Stone K 13, The Solar Year

At the top left hand corner of stone K 13, and reading from left to right, the five diamond shapes appear to have the upper half more deeply incised, the lower half less so. This is interpreted as five events: each comprising two halves; one heavy, one light, in other words five cycles of night time and day time. It can equally well be read as five nights and five days, a total of ten events equal to the ten vees. The two spirals may indicate the full day's sun on the first and fifth days, the concentric circles and hoop symbol below may mean

The Knowth Kerb Stone K13.

The incised markings on the kerb stone are clearly seen in the slanting light. The damaged portion of the stone at the top is noticeable; that part cannot be interpreted. *Photo:* Professor G. Eogan

many days, more than two days. The fifth diamond leads to and connects with a larger and slightly incomplete diamond with a horizontal attitude; this is interpreted as a whole unit, a 'week' of five days. A lead line runs parallel to one side for a short distance and then terminates at a figure of four concentric squares or 'weeks' implying a unit 'month' of twenty basic days. Adjacent and below is a further small double square, thought to mean two more days. On the right and at the edge of the damaged area are the vestiges of two vees which may have indicted two further days, thus making a possible total of twenty-four days, four fives plus four, the maximum number of days in a 'month'.

From the 'month' symbol, two parallel lines proceed towards the lower right in a zig-zag route, the last part of which has four triangles on one side, assumed to indicate a count of four; four months times four. The route ends in an enclosing diamond with a second internal diamond sub-divided into four. This symbol is assumed to indicate a whole year; within are the four quarters comprising the parts of the year.

A second zig-zag parallel path then commences leading to the beginning of a wavy line. The last diamond touches the wavy line, and within is a small spiral which may be supposed to be the symbol for start or commencement. Following the wavy line, a count will show there are sixteen bends and these are seen as the months of the year. The inverted vee of double lines between bends two and four defies explanation. At the eighth bend, a diamond with a dot in the centre touches the wavy line and this could be interpreted as the symbol for the half year.

After the sixteenth bend, and at the commencement of the long straight line, are a series of hoops. The exact number is uncertain because that part of the stone is damaged; an interpolation has however been made on the basis of spacing and sizes, and sixteen hoops is seen as a fair approximation of the correct number.

The number and proximity of sixteen hoops to the straight line is seen as a final re-statement of the number of months in a year.

The damage to the upper portion of the stone precludes the making of any deductions concerning the four smaller tight spirals and several individual remaining geometric figures. It is possible the left and right spirals may represent the summer and winter solstice, the centre pair of joined spirals the equinox events.

The entire design is assumed to be a statement of the relationships of days, weeks, months, quarters and the whole solar year of 365 days.

Kerb Stone K 14, The Symbolic Thirty-Three

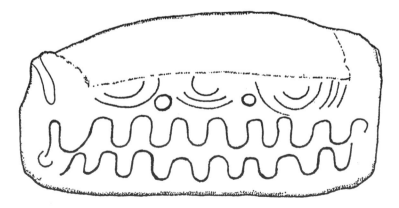

The wavy line seems to commence at the lower left and following the sequence, a total of thirty-three bends

Knowth Kerb Stone, K 15

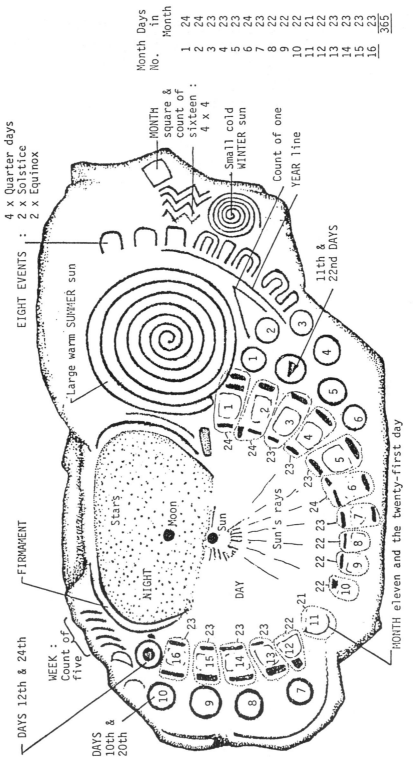

Month No.	Days in Month
1	24
2	24
3	23
4	23
5	23
6	24
7	23
8	22
9	22
10	22
11	21
12	22
13	23
14	23
15	23
16	23
	365

MONTH
square &
count of
sixteen :
4 x 4

Small cold
WINTER sun

Count of one

YEAR line

11th &
22nd DAYS

EIGHT EVENTS :   4 x Quarter days
2 x Solstice
2 x Equinox

Large warm SUMMER sun

DAYS 12th & 24th

WEEK :
Count of
five

FIRMAMENT

Stars

Moon

NIGHT

Sun

Sun's rays

DAY

DAYS
10th &
20th

MONTH eleven and the twenty-first day

Knowth Calendar

may be counted ending in a hoop at the extreme left.
The hoop is thought to signify the summation of the
group, the total, the whole, and each bend as a count
of one. The number is presumed to be a statement of
the symbolic number thirty-three and a means of
sanctifying the passage mound by such an affirmation.

Concerning the two small circles and the segments of
concentric curved lines above the wavy line, the two
passages into the Knowth mound are aligned in the
equinox sunrise and sunset so these two circles may
represent the equinox days. The curved lines may be
parts of spirals denoting the rising and setting sun on
these days.

Kerb Stone K 15, The Solar Calendar

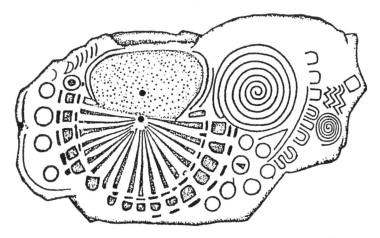

The stone is a unique statement; an exact 365 day, sixteen month, four week month, five day week solar
calendar. Refer to the Knowth Calendar on pages 42-
43.

The semi-circular group of squares is considered to
be a straight forward statement of the monthly divisions

of the year. All but one square has one, two or three groove marks immediately adjacent. On the basic month of twenty days, four weeks each of five days, it is assumed the squares are attributed with a value of twenty-one. The groove marks would then be the means of counting twenty-two, twenty-three and twenty-four as required. Summing the entire number, the total amounts to the 365 days of the solar year.

Five groove marks are to be seen above left, these are assumed to be the days of the week perhaps named Sunday, Moonday, Wodensday, Thorsday and Freyrday. Each named day would be repeated four times in twenty days, then called again for the other additional days each month.

Surrounding the semi-circle are ten plain circles presumed to be counted twice for the twenty basic days every month. The eleventh circle is marked by a small triangle and the twelfth has dot inside, this combination allowing the count and naming of the days beyond twenty to twenty-one and to twenty-four as required.

Reaching out to the semi-circle of squares, the radial lines are seen as the sun's rays shining forth from the sun just rising above the horizon. The sun is represented by the deep indentation in the centre. Above is the picked area of stone inside the concentric arced lines; in the middle is the moon, a deep indentation, and the stars are the picked marks. The twin arced lines presumably represent the firmament, the two lines indicating a solid shell or bowl upside down over the earth.

An ancient concept imagined the firmament was pricked with pin holes and the light shone through from the sun travelling around the Otherworld during our night time. Thus came starlight. This idea lacked the finesse of the much later Norse account of the creation of the world since it did not take into account the moving stars in their orbits. The Norse myth tells how Odin and his two brothers Vili and Ve took the burning embers from the realm of Muspell in the south and placed them in the sky, some were fixed in their places and others were to follow the paths ordained for them.

On the right hand half of the stone are two spirals; the larger has an anticlockwise rotation, is relatively large and is seen as the summer sun, bright and warm. The spiral terminates very close to the first 'month' square and this positional coincidence is presumed to mean the first month is synonymous with midsummer. Further to the right is a smaller tight spiral with clockwise rotation, seen as the dull cool winter sun. Between the two suns is a vee, a straight line and eight hoops. These are interpreted as a single year unit : one year sub-divided into eight anniversaries; four quarter days, two equinox and two solstice.

Immediately adjacent are four rows of zig-zag with four apices per row, a total of sixteen, and with a diamond close by. This group is interpreted as a re-statement of the sixteen months in one year.

The Knowth passage mound with its two passages aligned on sunrise and sunset at the equinox, the three incised kerb stones K 13, K 14 and K 15 is clearly a calendar building. It may be supposed to be the magic dwelling place of the calendar deity, the 'Brú' mound of the sun god.

The four calendar buildings in southern England were constructed nine and more centuries later, adhering to the same principles and fundamentals but to different geometric designs. The clear evidence of the considerable skills and effort required to construct these large calendar buildings must have reflected a firm belief in the value of such activities which had the general support of the entire population. That conviction linked with the mathematical form of the calendar points towards a live philosophy concerned with a solar calendar which developed some time before 3500 BC and probably lasted until Roman times and the advent of the Christian church and its missionary efforts from the first centuries AD.

Those of critical outlook may at this point express reservations concerning the hypothesis describing the sixteen month year and the weeks, the seasonal and quarterly events. To convince these sceptics, supporting argument is offered by way of a detailed description of the Mount Pleasant calendar building in appendix 2, commencing on page 95. Further reading of my *British Neolithic Calendar Buildings* will afford detailed explanations of the Sanctuary, Woodhenge and Stonehenge calendars. All these British designs have a common basis and match the Irish calendar point by point.

Calendars of Other Civilisations
It has been customery until now to attribute such civilised matters as a calendar almost exclusively to the Middle Eastern societies and the ancient civilisation of China. A search of the literature has enabled the tabulation below to be assembled in order to provide a

perspective to the claim that the Irish calendar of about 3500 BC is apparently the earliest evidence of man's attempt to measure the passing of the year in an accurate fashion. The approximate dates are given below of *definitive* archaeological or historical evidence equivalent to the Irish calendar, that is to say a comprehensive system of days, weeks, months and the solar year. The British calendar was also marked by the annual festivals which to a degree are still with us today.

NAME	TYPE	FORM	DATE
Irish	numerical solar	16 months of 21/24 days	Before 3500 BC, definitive
British	numerical solar	16 months of 22/23 days	Before 2600 BC, definitive
Egyptian	civil	12 months of 30 days + 5	Early third millennium BC
Sumerian	lunar		Uncertain, pre-Babylonian
Babylonian	lunar/solar	12 months	Early second millinnium BC
Chinese	lunar/solar	29/30 day month	Late second millennium BC
Indian/ Jewish/Greek	lunar/solar	29/30 day month	First millennium BC
Roman	numerical	12 months of 28/29/31 days	First millennium BC
Celtic	lunar	29/30 day month	First cent. BC
Julian	reformed Roman	12 months of 28/30/31 days	45 BC
Mayan	numerical	20 day months	First cent. AD
Gregorian	reformed Julian	12 months of 28/30/31 days	AD 1582

CHAPTER FOUR

STONE INSCRIPTIONS

Certainly the age of writing is the most
miraculous of all things man has devised.
Thomas Carlyle 1795-1881

Chapter two, 'The Symbols' and chapter three, 'The Calendar' provide an insight into the supposed ways the Irish symbols were used to record their ancient concept of the heavens and earth and their sixteen month calendar. It would be unfair to assert the list of symbols and the interpretation or meaning attributed to each was wholly correct unless it can be shown the symbol had wider application than just the Knowth kerb stones K 13, K 14, and K 15.

To provide evidence in support of this assertion, a further study of additional stone designs has been made. There is a considerable number of large stone monoliths used as kerb stones, wall stones, lintels, cap stones, and in other structural situations, that have incised designs carved upon them. In the pages to follow, a few additional examples are illustrated and the interpretations given. As each is considered it becomes clear the Irish symbols had consistency of form and presumably continuity of meaning.

The Newgrange Entrance Stone K 1, the Mid-winter Dawn Alignment

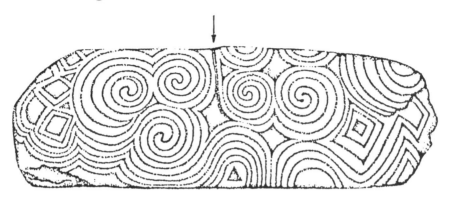

The passage which was constructed into the New-grange mound is about twenty metres in length and is aligned to coincide with the sun's rays at dawn on mid-winter's day. Outside the portal doorway are several massive kerb stones, the principal one is Newgrange K 1, the 'entrance stone', incised with a series of spiral designs and dual vertical lines. The latter aligns with and points towards the centre of the doorway and the direction of the passage.

To the left of the vertical lines are three anti-clockwise double-spirals, relatively large in overall size and these are presumed to represent the longer summer days. On the right are two clockwise double spirals, slightly smaller and supposedly representing the weak winter sun.

The vertical lines divide the two parts. Because they indicate direction, the alignment of the passage, it can be said to represent the bearing of dawn on mid-winter's day. Nearby, at the base of the stone, is a triangular mark which directs towards the vertical line, this may be a statement of one, that is to emphasise the single shortest day of the year, the mid-winter solstice. To the right is a diamond, close to the 'winter sun' and perhaps to form a statement of the unique event, the mid-winter's day dawn.

The remaining patterns appear to be purely ornamentation, not having any perceivable message or symbolism.

Acknowledging the calibrated construction date of 3200 BC for the Newgrange passage mound, it remains to be argued whether the incised rock designs were made at that time or at some much later date. No direct time assessment can be made of course, but by virtue of the vertical lines on Newgrange K 1 and K 52, also Knowth K 11 and K 74, which indicate specific solar alignments, it seems clear the designs were made at the same time as the mounds were built, otherwise the passage would not have been made on the chosen alignments.

In the case of K 1, the summer and winter sun symbols each side of the line can be linked with the deities Dagda and Oengus discussed in chapter five 'Legend and Myth', matters which tend to confirm the concept that Brú na Boinne (Newgrange by the River Boyne) was the dwelling place of the living sun god from the time of the mound's inception. The triple spiral design was probably the sun god's emblem.

Inside, the corbelled chamber walls at the end of the passage are formed from numbers of vertical stone slabs, the stone numbered L 19 has a repeat of the three double-spiral design incised upon it, and it is this stone which is illuminated by the dawn sun's rays on mid-winter day, a further confirmation of the mound's dedication to the sun god.

The three double-spiral motif could have been the specific symbol for the sun god; the inscription on K 1 would then be a declaration, a nameplate on the front door of the dwelling.

Newgrange Kerb Stone K 52, The Mid-Winter Dawn Alignment

To complement the entrance stone K1 and its relationship to the alignment of the passage and dawn on mid-winter's day, at the diametrically opposite position of the Newgrange passage mound can be seen kerb stone K 52. It too has spiral ornamentation and vertical parallel lines in the middle of the stone.

The three spirals comprise two larger clockwise designs and one smaller more tightly wound anti-clockwise spiral, supposedly representing the summer and winter suns. The directions of the two spirals are the same as those on the right-hand portion of the entrance stone K 1 on the opposite side of the passage mound.

The K 52 vertical line complements the vertical line on the entrance stone K 1 thus defining the mid-winter sunrise alignment passing through the passage mound.

To the right of the stone are three particularly notable symbols, each consisting of three circles surrounded by double lines roughly elliptical in shape. Other ornamentation further embellishes the stone. No success has been had interpreting any message presented by this part of the kerb stone. It is possible there may be a link between the three triple symbols and the later

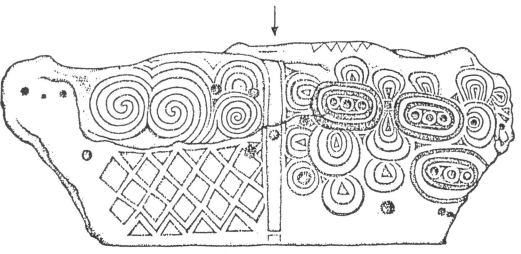

Newgrange Kerb Stone, K 52

historical use of the numbers three, nine and twenty-seven in Norse and Celtic folk tales. These numbers were used adjectivally to embellish the human attributes of character in a tale. By way of contrast, the numbers eleven and thirty-three were used to augment the descriptions of regal and Otherworld subjects.

Newgrange Roof Stone, East Chamber, Mid-Winter Solstice

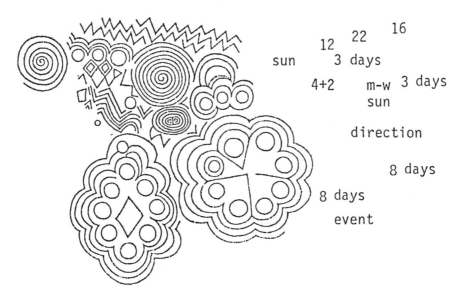

The account rests on the proposition that the first month of the year is that at mid-summer, thus the ninth month would be mid-winter. It also assumes the twelfth day of the first month is mid-summer sunrise, the twelfth day of the fifth month is the autumn equinox, the twelfth day of the ninth month is mid-winter's day, the twelfth day of the thirteenth month is the spring equinox. These characteristics of the same calendar are clearly shown at Mount Pleasant, England.

The incised design on the roof stone has been illustrated on the left and the interpreted numbers on the
right. To read the design, a narrative form of dialogue
has been chosen as a way of telling the message of the
stone, the story of the solstice by the 'priest' to his
'audience'. Because the sun rises in the east and travels
from left to right, the message has been read in the
same way; from left to right and from top to bottom:

The sun (⊚) rises every morning in all the sixteen
months (ⴍⴍⴍ). There are twenty-two days (ⴍⴍⴍ) in
the winter month. The twelfth (ⴍⴍⴍ) day is the sun's
(⊚) special event.

After the first three days (OOO) of the two fortnights
(twice two-weeks ◈) and two more (VV) days (O) of
the winter month, the 'high priest' commences his vigil,
watching and waiting at dawn for eight days (⦂°∴°)
before the special event, eleven days in all.

On the twelfth (〰️〰️) day (O) of the month is the
solstice, when the sun rises at its most southerly* direction (⊙⅃⊃) on the horizon. The dawn rays shine
directly on the sun god's (Oengus?) emblem, the triple
double spiral, at the entrance (K 1) and also on the wall
stone (L 19) within the innermost chamber, thus marking the solstice on mid-winter's day.

For eight more (⦂°°⦂) days (O) after the solstice, the
'high priest' watches at dawn each day as the light
shines into the passage. For three more days after that,
the sun illuminates the passage, until at the end of
eleven days after the solstice, the month ends and the
dawn's rays no longer light the passage of the 'Brú' of
the living sun god Oengus.

* The sunrise direction on the horizon (⊙⅃⊃) is the alignment
of the vertical inscription lines on Newgrange kerb stones K1
and K 52.

Knowth Kerb Stones K 11 and K 74,
Equinox Alignments

Linear designs are inscribed on the two Knowth kerb stones K 11 and K 74, respectively the entrance stones to the east and west passages to the mound, and diametrically opposite each other.

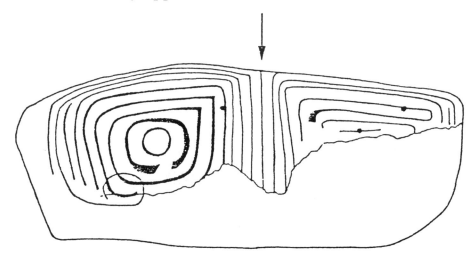

K 11 on the east side of the mound has a day (O) symbol surrounded by an artistic design. In the middle of the stone is a vertical line marking the equinox alignment. Because the established purpose of the mound was to recognise the equinox days, it is clearly logical to assert the incised design was accomplished at the same time the mound was built.

K 74 on the west side of the mound has a similar artistic design of horizontal and vertical lines as K 11, in this instance the equinox alignment of the setting sun is obviously shown by the twin vertical lines marked at the centre of the kerb stone, confirming the basic design intention of the mound builders.

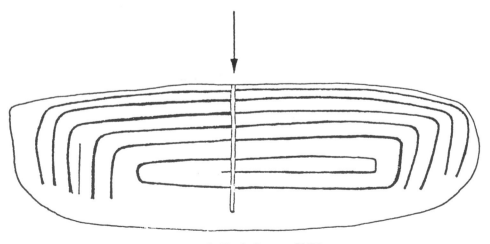

Knowth Kerb Stone, K 74

Knowth Kerb Stone K 36, The Four Seasons

To the left, the large circular symbol is believed to represent a single day, and then the extensive series of concentric hoops are seen as meaning the many, many, many days of the year.

Some damage has occurred on the top right hand corner of the stone but it is assumed a circle and hoop symbol indicates the symbol for a number of days. Next are two rows of wavy lines: three plus two, adding to the five changes of direction; this is considered to be a statement of the number of days, a count of five days of the week. Below, and between the three vertical parallel lines, are two vee patterns. The left hand design is interpreted as a count of four weeks leading to a diamond, seen as one whole month of four weeks. On the right side are four more vees and a diamond, thought to tell of four parts and a whole: four months comprising a whole 'quarter' of the year. The right-hand vertical line joins with the start of the route to be followed, the parallel zig-zag lines with four changes of direction. These four changes of direction are seen as counts of four; it appears there are four 'quarters' in a whole year. Next is the upright diamond presumably signifying an entity, that is the whole year. Within it is a smaller diamond divided into four parts, a symbol which could represent either four seasons or four quarters comprising the whole year.

The incised design is seen as a statement of the Calendar; the days, weeks, months and quarters of the sixteen month year.

Knowth Kerb Stone, K 36

Knowth Kerb Stone K 38, The Firmament

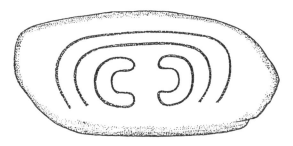

The kerb stone is at the southern end of the north-south alignment through the passage mound. To mark this characteristic of a mound whose principal feature is the east-west alignment, it would appear sensible to offer symbols indicating the sun's passage through the sky and dawn and dusk. The dual arc lines are thought to be a symbolic indication of the firmament and the sun's path across the sky, the two hoops representing the many sunrises and sunsets in the year, the beginning and end of each day.

Knowth Kerb Stone K 43, The Days and Months

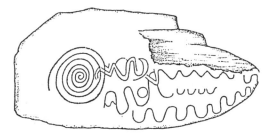

Reading the inscription by commencing at the upper left and then across to the right, the next line down and across, finally the bottom line, it is supposed the 'priest's' dialogue to his 'audience' would be:

The bright sun ( ) shines forth on us (parallel zig-zag lines) and on all humanity (nine bends). Five days (ᴖᴗᴡ) amount to one whole week (dual line vee) and there are four weeks (UUUU) in a month. There are sixteen months (sixteen bends) in a year and all humanity lives by our calendar.

Knowth Kerb Stone K 53, The Sun and Moon Months

The uppermost row of double circles is seen as a description of the moon in its various phases. Just below and central to that display are two sideways hoop symbols thought to indicate start and finish, in other words the grouping is a statement that the moon has a number of phases and it continually passes from one to another. Below this is a wavy line with twenty-nine bends; this is taken as a statement of the number of days in a moon's cycle of phases, the days in a lunar month. The actual period is 29.503 days as we know.

The sun symbol at the centre of the stone is a clear statement, it is traversed by a row of hoops and additional ones were drawn at both ends of the row, just as if the artist ran out of room and had to write up the page margin on each side. The total of twenty-two hoops is seen as a statement of the minimum number of days in every month of the sixteen month solar calendar.

The use of twenty-two hoop symbols to indicate the single days' count is an apparent contradiction with the chapter two listing of symbols and their meanings where a short stroke and a vee were attributed with the unit count, a group was represented by a hoop. Perhaps in this instance poetic licence was partly applied, the twenty-two double line hoops supposedly meant that this number of days occurred in each of the

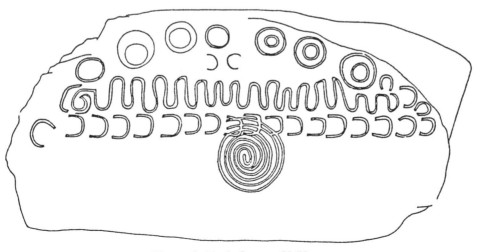

Knowth Kerb Stone, K 53

Knowth Kerb Stone, K 65

sixteen months of the year, thus affording a sense of plurality. Equally the double wavy line trace above is thought to have been a means of expressing that there were many lunar months in a year.

The kerb stone is presumed to have been a means of presenting comparative statements of the days in the solar and lunar months and to denote there were many months in a whole year.

Knowth Kerb Stone K 65, The Sun

The design on kerb stone K 65 has a simple story to tell, it is the pattern of the sun's behaviour every day:

Every day (O) of the week, on the first two days; Sunday and Moonday (◎), then also on the three days (◎), Wodensday, Thorsday and Freyrday, the sun rises and sets.

At dawn (⊂), the sun (◎) rises and begins its path across the sky. At mid-day, it reaches the highest point in the sky (◎) and its image is reflected in the waters of the river Boyne directly below (◎). The sun (◎) continues on its journey across the sky until dusk when the day ends (⊃), and its sinks below the horizon. Night, the time of darkness (҉)))) happens after the departure of the deity to the Otherworld.

Knowth Kerb Stone K 78, The Year

The idea being presented is interpreted as the relationship between the land and time, the seventeen provinces of Ireland and the sixteen month calendar.

The two abstract words, calendar and year, are not easy to portray in single symbols that have a pictorial theme. In the interpretation placed on the design K 78, these two words have been introduced. It is supposed

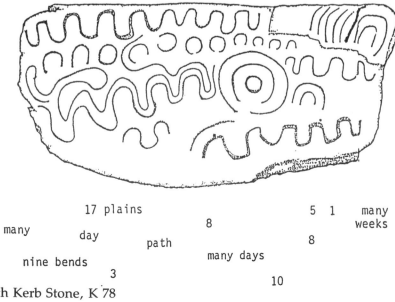

<pre>
              17 plains   5 1   many
                                    8   weeks
  many   day
                       path   8
      nine bends   many days
                3   10
</pre>

Knowth Kerb Stone, K 78

that the learned man, the 'priest', would explain the design to his 'audience' along the following lines, pointing to each symbol in turn to emphasise his verbal account. Commencing at the top left corner, in a clockwise direction:

> Our gods and ancestors have given us our land (seventeen bends); the Plain of Elta and sixteen newly cleared plains, and a calendar for all to know and live by. There are five days (((((() in one (/) week and many, many weeks in a month. There are eight lesser months (wavy line of eight bends) and eight festival months (eight hoops).
>
> The festivals are Summer solstice, the harvest thanksgiving to Lug,* Autumn equinox, Samain, Winter solstice, Imbolc, Spring equinox and the fertility festival of Beltane. Every (◎) day (O) our people join the processions (twin wavy lines of nine bends) to enjoy the many (∩ ∩) days (o) of festivities. The three festivals of Lug, Samain and Beltane are celebrated for ten (wavy line of ten bends) days, two weeks.
>
> * Use of the four more recent Celtic names for the ancient Irish festivals is intended to serve as an example only; perhaps one day we may know the true names, for clearly there were equivalent deities in those far off times.

The kerb stone K 78 is thought to have served as an advertising poster telling the general public of the relationships between the sacred calendar, the seventeen provinces and the people of Erin.

Knowth Kerb Stone K 79, The Universe

The interpretation placed on the Knowth kerb stone K 79 echoes that of the calendar stone K 15.

The lower left hoop symbol indicates the beginning (∩) of the story; the long line adjacent showing the idea of continuity ((⌐ᶫ)), of wholeness, leading the way

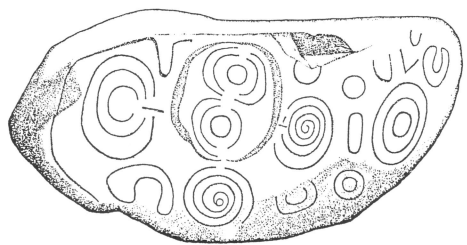

Knowth Kerb Stone, K 79

along. To the left are the three concentric hoops with a directional line (⟨ⓒ⟩) interpreted to mean many sun-rises illuminating man's world. On the right hand and opposite is the sun symbol also with a directional line, telling that the sun shines on this world of man every day. A second sun symbol below (◎) next to the 'start' symbol (⌒) implies the circular path of the sun around the Otherworld and outside the firmament (◯), first lighting this world and then sinking below the horizon and going further around to light the Nether-world below. The shaded picked semi-circular areas are interpreted as the firmament enveloping and surround-ing this world.

Within these arcs are two multiple symbols. The upper of the two (◎) is presumably a day (◯) in man's world and the lower part (◎) is the Nether-world below. The inner circles are seen as the day symbols and the semi-circles as dawn and dusk each day.

Having completed the interpretation of the left hand portion of the incised design and crossing to the right, these symbols are seen as representing the idea of the constantly renewed daily cycles.

One day (O) leads to (◖) two days (◉), Sunday and Moonday, and then to three days (◎), Wodens-day, Thorsday and Freyrday; then a vee (V) and two hoops (UU) meaning many days, and so on, round and round. Days come and go, life goes on and on. Lastly at the top right the 'finish' symbol (∪), signifying the completion of the story.

The whole design could have served as a blackboard diagram, aiding the teacher's instruction to his class of

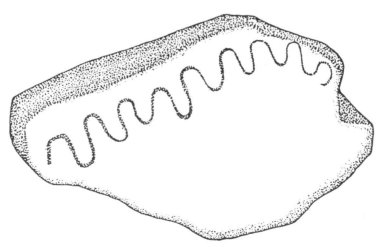

Knowth Kerb Stone, K 81

students in the mysteries of the movements of the sun's
movement in the heavens. A priest could have told the
story of the kerb stone K 79 along the following lines:

> The world we live in is on the top, the Netherworld
> is below. All is surrounded by the firmament. Each day
> the sun god begins his journey around the worlds, the
> light shines on us at dawn, then the sun goes down at
> the end of the day, passing down and underneath our
> world to reappear the next day.
>
> From one day (○) to (◊) the next, the two sky gods,
> Sunday and Moonday, are succeeded by the three
> deities, Wodensday, Thorsday and Freyrday, the whole
> making one (V) week (U), on and on. The end of one
> week is the beginning of the next, world without end.

Knowth Kerb Stone K 81, Seventeen

The seventeen bends in the wavy line are interpreted
as a simple statement of the symbolic number seventeen. Its symbolism is exemplified in the *Book of Leinster*
where a portion of the Mythological Cycle describes
how 'Partholan and Nemed between them cleared sixteen plains, which together with the "Old Plain of Elta"
fashioned by God before any invaders arrived, make a
total of seventeen.' The ancient *Book of Rights* describes
how seventeen kings accepted annual gifts from the
king of Cashel and there were seventeen kingdoms in
Meath.

Perhaps there were seventeen settlements in Ireland
in the third millennium, maybe a head chieftain at
Knowth and sixteen provincial vassal chiefs, all of
whom looked to Knowth for guidance and authority.
From these and other instances, it is clear the number
seventeen was associated with territorial matters. There
are also allied associations with kingdoms, rulers and

deities elsewhere in the Irish and Welsh legends. It is therefore reasonable to infer that the inscription on kerb stone K 81 is a symbolic statement of territorial and government matters.

The number seventeen is an indivisible prime number and is the midway value between one and thirty-three, which latter number is frequently used adjectivally to elevate a being, a place or occasion to regal heights. Seventeen would therefore appear to have a degree of regality, it would also seem to be a symbolic adjective with an implied sense of regality or divinity. The term 'year and a day' is sometimes used in a myth or legend to define how long the party of heroic voyagers stayed away or dwelt in another realm. The total time reaches into the seventeenth month, a year and the first month of the new year. This use of the term 'seventeen' gives an added lustre to their adventures and a touch of the Otherworld.

Loughcrew, Slieve na Calliagh, The Calendar Stone

About 40 km west of the Boyne mounds is the Loughcrew area, the hills of the witch. The eastern hill has a stone circle near its crest, the references describe it as 'cairn X'. A ring of eight stones surrounds the centre stone which is about one metre in width. The concave side containing the incised design faces north. The symbols are similar to those on Knowth kerbstone K 15. (See page 72.)

Interpreting the design from left to right, the circle at the lower left is thought to be the sun, that at the upper centre the moon. The twin arc lines are seen as the shell of the firmament surrounding the earth, man's domain is at the centre, the radiating lines indicating the firma-

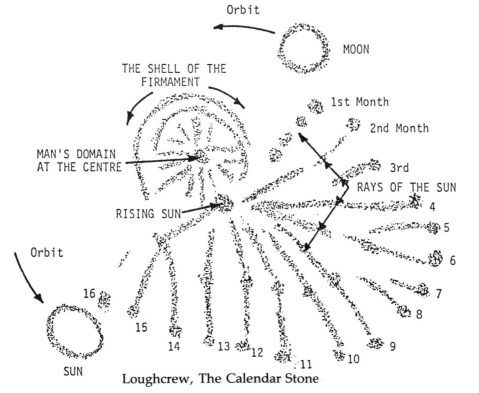

Loughcrew, The Calendar Stone

ment can be seen in all directions.

The rising sun is the deep depression at the centre, from which are seen radiating lines, admittedly somewhat irregular in arrangement, which lead to an inner ring of small depressions and then out further to the sixteen slightly deeper depressions totalling sixteen altogether.

The story to be told would clearly be very similar to the Knowth account; the sixteen months of the year, the sun rises at dawn to shine on each new day. The sun and the moon circle around in the Otherworld outside the firmament, man's domain is lit during the day, and at night the light shines through the small holes in the firmament to become the stars.

The similarity of the two designs at Slieve na Calliagh and Knowth points towards a common philisophy for two distant communities, that each was contemporary with the other about 3500 BC.

Loughcrew Cairn F, Stone C1, The Lunar Months

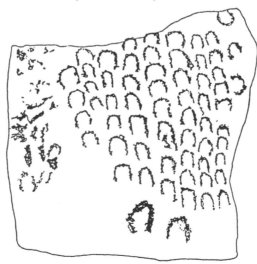

Loughcrew, Slieve na Calliagh

The simple inscription on Cairn F stone C1 shows nine vertical columns of hoops. Accepting that each hoop represents a group of events, in this instance the number of days in a lunar month, the total of sixty-two hoops multiplied by 29.503 days per lunar month equals 1,829.2 days. This period compares with five solar years of 365.25 days per year, a total of 1,826.3. The insignificant difference of three days in five years does not detract from the assertion that the stone design appears to be a statement of the number of lunar months in five solar years.

From the presence of such a design, it may be inferred the ancient inhabitants of Ireland had a lunar calendar of 29/30 day months at the same time as a solar calendar of sixteen months of 22/23 day or 21/24 day months very early in their settlement of the country. The declaration on C1 would seemingly be a public statement of the relationship between the two calendrical systems.

Fournocks Passage, Thirty-Three

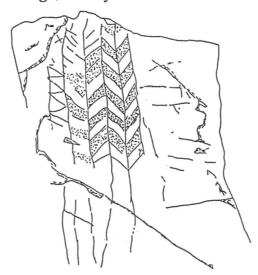

Of significance in the collection of patterns and designs inscribed on the Fourknocks passage stones is one monolith which is particularly worthy of examination.

There are six vertical lines with chevron patterns between. Standing back for a moment and taking a critical view of the inscriptions, it appears there are two differing standards of execution. The three vertical columns in the centre seem to have been made by one person. The two columns to the left have a quite haphazard appearance and may have been added later, they are away from the centre of the stone and are not balanced by any inscriptions on the blank right hand side.

Concentrating the discussion on the three central columns, it can be seen each has eleven parallelograms, some picked and others unornamented. The significant count of three columns each of eleven, a total of thirty-three, is particularly important.

The same number was represented on the Knowth kerb stone K 14 and has been used in folktales to embellish a story as late as the Welsh *White Book of Rhydderch* in the fourteenth century AD. Both three and eleven separately were equally symbolic, the multiplicant thirty-three particularly so. It has frequently been used to imply supra-human attributes, regal authority and deification.

The left hand portion of the incised design, presumably added at a later date, has insufficient coherence to permit a logical interpretation and the development of an hypothesis concerning its meaning. The central portion of the design is thought to be an affirmative statement of the number thirty-three, a means of asserting the stone and that its immediate area was associated with the deities; in other words the place was a sacred site. It is equally possible the site was the place of the king, the seat of government, either of one of the provincial kings or of the principal ruler.

Postscript

If you visit the toys' and games' shop in your neighbourhood shopping centre, I expect you will readily find a board game called 'cat and mice' or 'fox and geese'. It used to be popular in Viking times as 'hnefatafl' and earlier in the Welsh hills when it was called 'gwyddbwyll'.

The thirty-three peg holes or hollows are intended to receive the playing pieces; seventeen mice or geese and one cat or fox. The players are allowed to move their pieces up and down the board or sideways across the board, in the process endeavouring to take the pieces of the opponent.

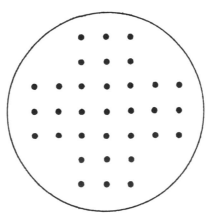

Solitaire Board

The board can also be used to play 'solitaire' where thirty-two balls and one empty space allow the player to gradually eliminate all the balls except one.

One can wonder at the antiquity of these games based upon the same symbolic numbers as the ancient Irish passage mound designs.

CHAPTER FIVE

Legend and Myth

*To know the myths is to learn the secret
of things. In other words, one learns not
only how things came but also where to
find them and how to make them reappear
when they disappear.*

Mircea Eliade 1907-

The Irish Myth

'The oldest existing literature of any people north of the
Alps' is the description of an assembly of ancient Irish
stories collected and written about AD 1100 by Irish
monks and scribes. The *Book of Leinster* is the most well
known of all the volumes. The tales generally tell of
events between 200 BC and AD 300 but some of the
legends clearly refer to very much earlier times. Our
immediate concern is with the group of tales known as
the 'Mythological Cycle' and their relevance to the
passage mounds within the bend of the River Boyne
and other related places of the ancient times in Ireland.

The Invasions

It is a matter of note that there is no story of the creation
of the world or of man's domain in Irish mythology.
Instead the twelfth century Irish manuscript *The Book of
the Conquests*, the *Lebor Gabala*, contains a number of
episodes describing the six invasions of Ireland in past
ages, long before the coming of Saint Patrick and

Christianity in the period AD *c.* 389–*c.* 461.

The Book tells how Keasir and her followers came first to Ireland in ancient times and dwelt in the land.

The second invasion came many hundreds of years later with Partholan and his followers. They fought with and defeated the Fomore, a race of sea giants then living in Ireland. Winning these contests, the Partholan settled the land; they were the first people to brew beer, to work gold, to have domesticated cattle and a cooking cauldron, to have law-givers and ritual ceremonies. The Partholan people lived in peace until in later ages they were defeated by the plague.

These statements tend to indicate the immigration of a socially civilised people, who defeated the indigenous natives then leading nomadic lives on the island. Whether the newcomers were of the stone age or later is indeterminate.

Nemed and his people then arrived in the country, living in peace and harmony, until in their turn they were conquered by the Fomore, the sea giants. The Nemed were compelled to pay annual tribute to their giant overlords. The Nemed suffered great privations and ultimately fled the country, to return again much later.

The fourth invasion by the returning Nemed and their allies comprised three companies; the Fir Bolg, the Gallioin and the Fir Domnan. The first name is reminiscent of the name of the Belgae tribe who lived on the Continent, roughly in the area we now know of as Belgium. The two latter names have phonetic similarities with Gaul, that part of northern France and Brittany, also the Dumnonii tribe in south-west Britain. The consonance of the three names points towards firm links with France, Brittany and England and an instance of one of the many migrations of the north-western peoples from one location to another. How far back in time is difficult to answer. It has been said an examination of the Fir Bolg 'raths' (= barrows) at Moytura, County Mayo, has revealed only stone implements, establishing that the Fir Bolg were of the Irish stone age period, preceding the bronze age commencement about 1500 BC.

The followers of the Bolg were some time later subjected to an invasion from the north by the Tuatha de Danann, the 'Peoples of the Goddess Danann'. The Tuatha were a people possessed of magic wonders, the supreme artists of wizardry, who came to Ireland, not by ship, but descended from the northern sky. They dwelt in a timeless land of everlasting festivities, a supernatural realm, the domain of the gods. Their mythological sites of the Otherworld, the 'Brú', were magic places not inhabited by humans. The Brú na Boinne (Newgrange by the river Boyne) was the most important of these places.

The composition and manner of telling the legends concerning the Tuatha and their deities, Dagda and Oengus, make it clear the new arrivals adopted Brú na Boinne as their own, attributing to it their own gods and myths. That they were credited with magic wonders and the like is indicative of two things. Firstly, it could be a way of raising the early Irish settlers status to that of gods, but on a more prosaic level it could explain the difference between the stone age and bronze age peoples, their outlook and attitudes of those times. The higher degree of deification earned by the Tuatha would probably have arisen from a far longer period of settled life and peaceful existence, the two elements being linked in that way.

The next and sixth invaders were the Sons of Mil, the Milesians, who took Ireland from the Tuatha shortly before Christianity came to the country. It seems probable the Irish Milesians could have been the European people we know of as the Celts. Their population movements across Europe to Britain and Ireland occurred partly as a result of the Roman Empire expansion in the centuries BC. It is on record the European Celts were a warlike and aggressive people. Alternatively, it is equally possible the Milesians could have derived from Britain as a result of the Roman conquest of that country. They could have been defeated and displaced British tribes escaping to the west in the first century AD. Whatever their origins, they clearly absorbed and handed on the ancient Irish folklore and myth to succeeding generations.

The transition from pre-history to history takes us to the conversion of the Irish peoples to Christianity by Saint Patrick in the period AD *c.* 389–*c.* 461. There would have been a gradual displacement of the old beliefs, the legends and myths of old. It has been our good fortune they were committed to paper before being forgotten.

Thirty-Three
In Rees' book *Celtic Heritage* there is quoted the following selections from the Irish tales:–

Thirty-two leaders of the Tuatha de Danann are listed in the first battle of Mag Tuired, and this does not include Lug their saviour in the second battle. With them may be compared the company of thirty-three men, all seemingly thirty-two years of age who sit at the tables in the Otherworld island castle in Perlesvaus. Nemed reached Ireland with only one ship; thirty-three were lost on the way. Cuculainn slays thirty-three of the Labriads in the Sid (Brú), and a late account of the second battle of Mag Tuired names thirty-three leaders of the Fomore, thirty-two plus their high king. . .

Elsewhere I have described the numerous occasions where the number thirty-three is incorporated into ancient monument designs and is used adjectivally in tales and legends. Two particularly notable instances are the wavy lines on the Knowth kerb stone K 14, also the preceding references quoted by Rees. In practically every case examined, a little thought reveals the storytellers' intention of indicating the supreme importance of the place or person described, a sense of regality, of the Otherworld. That the Knowth stone was inscribed with the symbolic value so long ago, also the Fourknocks passage stone similarly, shows the great antiquity of the idea.

The most recent example detected is incorporated in the geometric design of the Arthurian building dated c. AD 600 at Cadbury Castle, Somerset, England. The length and breadth wall lengths sum to thirty-three megalithic rods.

The symbolic use of thirty-three is one example of north-west European culture and its great antiquity; our contemporary celebrations marking May Day, 1 August and Hallowe'en are the quarter day anniversaries of the sixteen month calendar, further instances of the continuity of belief and practice.

The Deities

Elcmar was supposedly the first deity to dwell in New-grange and was married to the divinity Boand (the River Boyne). Little is known about the nature of this deity. The myths attribute magical and mystical powers to the river, its source is supposed to be an Otherworld well surrounded by a grove of hazel trees. The hazel nuts fall into the river forming bubbles of mystic inspiration. The river is sometimes called the 'Brú of the woman of Elcmar'.

In later ages, the all powerful and good god Dagda tricked Elcmar by sending him on an errand for a day. This period was magically lengthened to nine months and during this time Boand had a son by Dagda 'who was begotten at the break of day and born betwixt it and the evening'. Their son Oengus is regarded as the personification of the day. He succeeded his father and the ancient literature has many references to the Brú of Oengus, meaning the magic mound and the super-natural home of Oengus. It is the most widely used term describing the Newgrange passage mound in the myths. For this fundamental reason I hold the firm opinion some archaeologists are in error by usually referring to these three mounds as 'burial mounds' and 'grave mounds'; the lesser mounds may have been burial places for worldly men but these three sacred mounds are associated with the deities of old, they were not primarily places of burial. As late as AD 1084 Tigernach's *Annals* assert Oengus was alive and well in his 'Brú'.

The statement that the Tuatha de Danann arrived from the north, linked with the name of the deity

Oengus who succeeded Dagda, brings to mind the popular Scottish name Angus and the proximity of south-west Scotland to the northern part of Ireland. Which name came first is a matter of conjecture. Were the Tuatha early Scots who invaded Ireland and imposed their own deity in place of Dagda, adding to the myth to explain the substitution of Elcmar by Dagda and then by Oengus.

As a people, the Tuatha became elevated to deities as generation succeeded generation, gradually becoming attributed with their powers in myth and folklore.

The legends mention the (Celtic) god Lug as a latecomer to their cycles, partly replacing the god Oengus. In contrast with the earlier deities who were presented as beneficient, old and wise, Lug is portrayed in the Celtic manner as a young and handsome man, armed with the superior weapons, the sling and the spear, an all efficient and aggressive deity. This grafting of a Celtic god onto the ancient tales could have occurred at the time of the Milesian invasion. In the centuries before Christianity, the legendary person could have become deified and incorporated into folklore.

Pre-History
Reflecting on the tale which says the Nemed suffered great privations and ultimately abandoned the country, it is likely that the event was actually a series of crop failures, a natural disaster of several years duration. Whilst it was said to be the result of a battle with the demons, there is the likelihood it was a natural occurrence such as the effect of climatic changes resulting from the explosion of the volcano Santorini just

north of the Mediterranean island of Crete in 1626 BC. Colossal clouds of dust were hurled into the atmosphere causing lower than normal temperatures to occur because the sun's energy was blanketed and warmth failed to reach the earth in the northern hemisphere. The sub normal climatic conditions during the growing seasons caused tree growth to be inhibited and dendrologists have detected narrower than normal tree ring growth at that time.

In those circumstances, crops would have failed, cattle would have little to eat and the people of the land would have suffered great privations. To attribute such circumstances to the anger of the gods and to a war between the good and demonic deities would have been understandable. Thus the probable source of the myth.

The most recent prehistoric tale concerns the king of Ireland immediately before the arrival of Christianity, an extract from which is as follows:–

> Mag Slecht, whence was it named? It is there the king idol of Ireland was, i.e. Crom Croich, and the twelve idols around him, but he was of gold. And until the coming of Patrick he was the god of every people that occupied Ireland.

The description refers to a circle of standing stones with a central obelisk, the manner of telling implying the elevated status of the king represented by the account.

Christianity

Patrick's conversion of the Irish people to Christianity has been dated from AD *c.* 389 to *c.* 461, marking the introduction of Latin and the written word. In the first couple of centuries the monks wrote in Latin but as time

A CHRONOLOGY OF ANCIENT IRISH GODS AND THE INVASIONS

Event	Date	Description
Knowth	*3500 BC	The passage mound built with aspects of the solar sixteen month calendar and symbolic numbers.
Newgrange	*3200 BC	
First Invasion		Keasir and her followers settled the land.
Second Invasion	2500 BC	Partholan and his men; perhaps Elcmar the sun god was their deity.
Third Invasion	2000 BC	The first Nemed invasion; Dagda the Good god?
Eruption of Santorini island	*1625 BC	Poor harvests and privations, perhaps for a year or two.
Fourth Invasion	1500 BC	The Fir Bolg, the Gallioin and the Fir Domnan with the Nemed. Dagda the Good god. Introduction of soft bronze and metalworking.
Fifth Invasion	1000 BC	The Tuatha de Danann and the advent of Oengus who displaced Dagda. The introduction of hard bronze and better tools.
Sixth Invasion	300 BC	The Sons of Mil who may have been the Celts. The deity Lug displaces earlier names.
Crom Croich	300 AD	The king of all Ireland at the time.
Christianity	*400 AD	Saint Patrick the celebrated missionary converts Ireland to the Christian beliefs.

* Established dates are shown by the *, others are hypothetical but are based on reasoned argument and the mythological accounts

wore on they began to record the myths and legends in the native Irish language. It is from these records that we have an ability to attempt a review of the past.

Ages and Invasions

Gathering together the pieces of evidence, supported by hints and other clues to the past, linking these with what we know about the three passage mounds New-grange, Knowth and Dowth, it is worthwhile to formulate a chronological table of the invasions and their deities. Some adjustments may have to be made in the future, but in the meantime the best estimate of dates and events is given in the accompanying table.

The Viking Myth of the Creation of the World

Snorri Sturlusson was a notable Icelandic chieftain and scholar who lived in Iceland in the twelfth century. He recorded many old Norse sagas and myths, the tales of the old gods before Christianity came to Iceland in AD 1000. Amongst these was *The Deluding of Gylfi* in the *Prose Edda* written about AD 1220.

This, the Norseman's myth of the creation of the world, has a very special interest for us. It was told this way:

> In the beginning there was nothing, the great emptiness that was the realm of Ginnungagap. Then Niflheim was made, the realm of the north, a place of ice and covered in snow. In the midst of it was a well from which flowed eleven rivers: cool, defiant, bubbling, fearsome, storming, broad, fast, freezing, and three more, clear waters flowing into the void. Then Muspell was made in the south, a land of light, of heat and burning flame, able to be endured only by those born there. On guard is Black Surt armed with his blazing sword. At the end of

the world he will vanquish all the gods and burn the whole world with fire. Mountains will fall, the heavens will be rent apart, and mankind will tread the road to Hel.

The eleven rivers streamed into the emptiness and the spray from the flowing waters turned to rime, the froth turned to ice and layer formed on layer. The northern part of the realm was covered in ice and hoar frost, beset by skuthers of cold wind. The southern part was warmed by the heat of Muspell and lit by the sparks and glowing embers. In the middle was mildness and windless air, the soft air of the heat meeting the thawing and dripping ice of the north.

Life formed from the flowing liquid and grew into the evil frost giant Ymir.

From the thawing of the frost came a cow named Adumla and four rivers of milk flowed from her teats which fed Ymir. And she licked the ice layers which were salty and on the third day a whole man was revealed named Buri. His son called Bor married Bestla and their three sons were Odin, Vili and Ve.

The assembly of brutal frost giants led by Ymir were hated and their behaviour eventually led the three brothers to kill Ymir. They carried the body to the middle of the great emptiness and made the world from him. The seas and lakes they made from the rivers of his blood. And after they had made the earth they laid the turbulent ocean all around, so wide that few men would try to cross it.

Because of the other ogres' hostility, Bor's sons used Ymir's eyebrows to build an enclosed stronghold called Midgard. There the sun warmed the earth and it was green with sprouting leeks.

They lifted Ymir's skull and placed it so the four corners reached the ends of the earth and the sky was formed above.* Under each corner they placed a dwarf to hold up the sky and their names were East and West and North and South.

Odin, Vili and Ve were walking along the strand one day and they came upon two trees which had fallen. One was an ash and the other an elm. Bor's sons lifted them up and made them into the first man and woman; Odin breathed into them and gave them the spirit of life, Vili gave them sharp wits and feeling hearts, Ve gave them hearing and sight. And the man was named Ask after the ash tree, and the woman was named Embla after the elm tree.

And they were given Midgard to live in. All the families and races and nations of man are descended from them.

And the earth was made this way, surrounded by the sea and covered by the sky, inhabited by men and giants and dwarfs. And Odin and the other gods then built their own realm of Asgard high above Midgard. It is a place of green plains and shining palaces, a stronghold in the sky. The two regions are linked by the brilliant rainbow bridge.

* See pages 23 and 24. Apart from the several other elements of the Viking creation story, it is important to realise the basic concept of the inverted dome over man's domain, the firmament above the sky. Such a fundamental idea could well have been in the minds of the ancient Irish peoples, and could clearly be drawn as the twin arcs above the rays of the sun portraying the months.

A Last Word

What is befitting as a closing comment? I set out with the objective of deciphering the ancient Irish stone inscriptions, having been prompted by a television programme concerning the Australian aborigines and their art.

Mention was made of the successes had by philologists in deciphering the ancient Middle Eastern scripts where dual language inscriptions were found. In the instance of the Boyne valley inscriptions, the link has been the later British sixteen month calendar, the behaviour of the sun and the moon.

I can see many 'wise' heads being shaken in disbelief, saying the interpretations of the symbols and the calendrical assertions are too fanciful to be true because the ancient Irish were only just removed from the primitive state. That kind of opinion is often cited by so-called experts in order to establish their superiority and thus the respectibility of their theories in preference to others.

My researches are based on fact and the logical development of an hypothesis, not on opinions.

Realisation came when wider reading and research brought together pieces of the jigsaw to reveal a fairly complete picture. It was important to link the legends and myths with the archaeological record, to identify the key ideas, to bring together and to present a coherent whole.

You, the reader, may judge the degree of success I have had in interpreting the ancient Irish art and its relationship to their calendar and myths. You may also wish to form your own assessment of the skills and knowledge of the forebears of today's Ireland, the land of Erin.

APPENDIX ONE

Dates and Dating

Radio Carbon Dating

All carbonaceous materials such as wood, antlers and fibres contain carbon, and of the total a very small proportion is the radioactive isotope usually abbreviated to C_{14} or C14. The carbon isotope is formed by the action of cosmic rays colliding with the nitrogen atoms in the outer atmosphere, the isotope eventually becoming included in living matter. When the subject dies no more radioactive carbon is received into the piece of wood or whatever else. From that time on it is practical to assess the date of the specimen by measuring the gradually reducing level of C14 as the isotope reverts back to nitrogen. The half-life of C14 is about 5,730 years meaning the level of radiation reduces in that time to half the previous amount. Using the sample's weight as a measurement basis an estimate of its age can be made, calculated from the time the radioactive isotope ceased to be absorbed into the living tissue.

The 'carbon' dates are accompanied by an indication of their statistical accuracy, e.g. 3500 ± 130 years bp means the age of 3500 years *before* the *p*resent is correct to within a 50% chance of 130 years either way. This may be interpreted as:

3500 ± 130 − AD 1950 = 1550 bc ± 130 years.

The AD 1970 report by Professor H. E. Seuss of La Jolla Laboratory in California, USA, showed radioactive carbon dates were in error the greater the age of the specimen. He related the ages of successive generations of bristle cone pine trees from the White mountains in California by counting the yearly growth rings and the C14 ages. Abbreviating his graph of calibration corrections, the approximate adjustments are given in the table below. The BC date, the correct 'calibrated date' is obtained by adding the correction of say 300 years to the bc date, e.g.:

$$3500 \text{ bp} - 1950 = 1550 \text{ bc} + 300 = 1850 \text{ BC}$$

Dates quoted in this volume are either historical, calibrated or a reasonable approximation based upon related data.

Carbon 14 bp	Date bc	Calibration Correction	Calibrated Date AD/BC
0		0	AD 2000
500		0	AD 1500
1000		0	1000
1500		0	500
2000	—	0	0
2500	500	+100	600 BC
3000	1000	+200	1200 BC
3500	1500	+300	1800
4000	2000	+400	2400
4500	2500	+500	3000
5000	3000	+650	3650
5500	3500	+750	4250
6000	4000	+850	4850
6500	4500	+900	5400
7000	5000	+1000	6000

Abbreviations

The conventional dating nomenclature has been followed in preparing the text, and it is well to state these for the reader who may be slightly less familiar with the subject:

BC   the initials as capitals and without full stops are intended to mean Before Christ (the accepted date of his birth). They may equally be interpreted as BCE, Before the Common Era, a convention used by other than Christian societies and meaning the same reference date.

bc   the lower case initials refer to radioactive carbon dates before the reference date.

bp   the lower case initials refer to radioactive carbon dates before the present.

AD   the capital initials before the number and without full stops mean Anno Domini, the Latin for 'the year of our Lord', i.e. since the birth of Christ. The equivalent abbreviation is CE, the Common Era, to the same reference date, e.g. AD 1987 equals CE 1987.

c   the abbreviation for 'circa', the Latin for approximately.

APPENDIX TWO

The Mount Pleasant Calendar

The Mount Pleasant timber building, circular in shape and nearly forty metres diameter, was erected about 2600 BC (4058 ± 71 years bp, BM 792) and comprised 183 oak posts, sixteen of which were half a metre in diameter and the remainder averaging a little less. The posts were arranged in rings and sub-divided into four quadrants by avenues. At the centre were four upright stone columns in a square, in between were slabs on edge enclosing the area about six by six metres.

A reconstruction of the design is shown in the figure overleaf. The diagonals of the central square divide the four quadrants into eight sectors, so that by counting all the posts and sectors twice, a tally equal to the number of days in a year and sixteen sectors is reached. In other words, 365 days and sixteen months. The grouping of the inner ring of sixteen posts, the month posts, when considered in relation to the next ring of posts, three per sector, serves to count the days of a week. The next ring of posts in every odd numbered month sector is assumed to be the second week of five days. Subsequent weeks were counted in successive rings of posts.

To arrive at the number of months and days in a year, the arithmetical process of halving was used as a means of division. Commencing by subtracting the odd day of the year, the 365th, then halving the 364 days gives a half year of 182 days, halving again makes four quarters

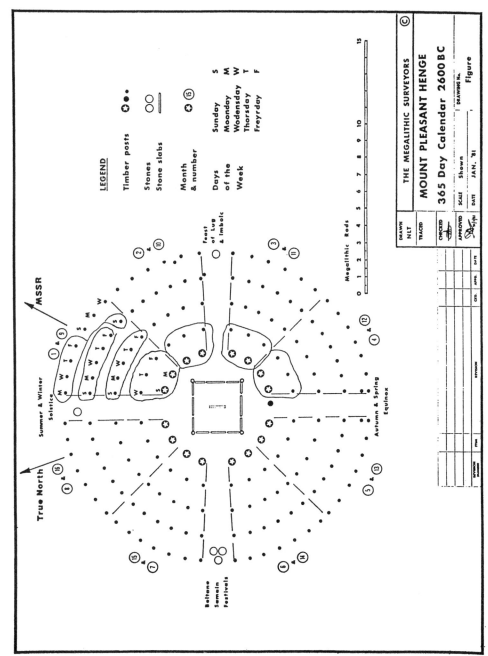

Mount Pleasant Calendar

of 91 days. Next, each quarter can be conveniently sub-
divided into four 'months' of 23, 23, 23 and 22 days.
The posts in each sector of the design testify to this process of thought as reference to the figure will show. The
sequence of days and months is believed to have been:

Month Number	1	2	3	4	5	6	7	8	9	10	11	12	13	14	15	16		

Days of
Month   23 23 22 23 23 23 23 22 23 23 22 23 23 23 23 22   = 364
                                        Plus the 365th day =   1
                                        Total days in the year = 365

Further halving of each month into two 'fortnights' and
again into four 'weeks' would have enabled the calendar designer to arrive at the convenient unit of a five
day week. Two or three intercalary days had to be
added at the end of each twenty day cycle to complete
the month of 22 or 23 days.

The arrangements of the sixteen posts, the sectors,
the quadrants, the grouping of posts in fives and the
dual rotation of counting in a full year account for all
the design elements.

Names of the months and days have been proposed
on page 37 and these are quoted in the figure to assist
in explaining how the 365 day calendar was constructed
and operated.

No provision was apparently made for the additional
day needed in a leap year nor for the varying declina-
tion of the sun which results in unequal numbers of
days in the half years between equinox events. This
would have required an adjustment in the number of
twenty-three day months with the creation of twenty-
four day summer months and also a corresponding

increase in the number of twenty-two day months in the winter.

The basic principles of the calendar design are thought to have incorporated the following:—

(*a*) The total number of posts used to construct the building was 183; two complete counting circuits of the building were required each solar year, twice 182 plus one equals 365 days.

(*b*) The four quadrants of the design represented the four quarters of the year. In each quadrant, four large posts tallied the four months in a quarter, each month post was counted successively to tell the full sixteen months of the full year.

(*c*) The days of the week in each month were indicated by markers on the twenty-two or twenty-three posts of the eight sectors. The first two days of the week, Sunday and Moonday, were counted on the large posts followed by Wodensday, Thorsday and Freyrday on the three posts of the next row. The second week was counted on the third row of posts, Sunday to Freyrday inclusive. The succeeding days and weeks are assumed to have continued in sequence until at the end of the fourth week the two or three additional days were counted to complete the month.

The causeway entrance to Mount Pleasant was from a northerly direction on the line of the north south avenue. The bearing of dawn on mid-summer's day, about 50° east of north, bisects the first sector. This feature led to the idea that the twelfth day of month one was mid-summer's day, the middle day in twenty-three, the middle day in the summer month so to speak. This reference has been adopted as the start of the calendar.

Progressing clockwise around the pattern of posts, it will be seen that no division exists between months one and two, but the eastern avenue occurs between months two and three. A compression indication of a stone marker was detected at this spot. At the southern end of the north south avenue, no marker was found but a stone has been assumed since it was likely erosion had occurred. In the western avenue three compression marks were found. The northern avenue also had the compression mark of a stone. These occurrences of markers in the avenues are assumed to have indicated special events beginning in the third, seventh, eleventh and fifteenth months. Considering these in relation to the four seasons of the year in months one, five, nine and thirteen, a reconstruction of the prehistoric calendar was attempted. The table on page 101 'Calendar Events Comparison' illustrates the 2600 BC calendar alongside the 1987/88 calendar. The stones in the avenues occur on dates we know now as the ancient Celtic festivals of Lug, Samain, Imbolc and Beltane which are amply documented in historic Irish, Welsh and Scottish literature. In modern day terms the ancient festivals equate with 1 August, 1 November, 1 February and 1 May.

The marker stones can be interpreted as occurring after the last day of the previous month and before the first day of the next, in other words, during the hours of darkness between sunset and sunrise. Assuming the festivals began on the first day of the new month, by the fifth day the events could have reached a climax.

These dates match today's 1 May, Mayday in Britain and St Walburg's night in Germany (a witches night); 1 August, August Bank holiday in England and a Swiss national holiday; Halloween on 31 October and Candlemas on 1 February. We also celebrate New Year's Eve at midnight and this coincides with the last day of month nine, the cold winter month.

The solstitial and equinoctial events are interpreted slightly differently. The Calendar Comparisons indicates they were on the twelfth day of the month, the middle of twenty-three days in months one, five, nine and thirteen. These middle nights were the longest, the shortest and the days with equal hours of daylight and darkness. The idea of the 'twelfth night' would have loomed large in the minds of the sun worshippers as those days approached. In our Christian calendar, the twelfth night is the festival of Epiphany after Christmas. One can speculate at the possible absorption of folklore tradition as Christianity successfully appealed for men's minds.

These eight principal events were clearly the cornerstones of the year. The mathematical elegance of sixteen months, sixty-four weeks, four solar events and four quarters of the year is quite apparent. One must admire the ability of the men who conceived this ingenious method of measuring the year and its progress.

The number nine has strong links with Woden or Odin, the ancient British and Norse deities. At the end of the ninth month, it is feasible there was a celebration of some kind to mark the end of the shortest month, an appeal to Woden or his equivalent, for his protection in the months to come. That night coincides with New

Mt Pleasant Calendar, 2600 BC   Today's Calendar

	Mt Pleasant month/days			Today month/days
North avenue stone				J 30
Midsummer sunrise First month, middle & 12th day	1	23	Solstice June 21st	
	2	23		J 31
East avenue stone Lugnasad festival Third month, 1st to 5th days	3	22	Lammas day August 1st	A 31
	4	23		
South avenue stone absent				S 30
Autumn Fifth month, middle & 12th day	5	23	Equinox September 23rd	
	6	23		O 31
West avenue stones Samain ceremonies Seventh month, 1st to 5th days	7	23	Hallowe'en October 31st	N 30
	8	22		
North avenue stone				D 31
Midwinter sunrise Ninth month, middle & 12th day, Woden ceremonies?	9	23	Solstice December 22nd New Year's Eve New Year's day	
	10	23		J 31
East avenue stone Imbolc anniversary Eleventh month, 1st to 5th days	11	22	Candlemas day February 1st	F 28
	12	23		
South avenue stone absent				M 31
Spring Thirteenth month, middle & 12th day	13	23	Equinox March 20th	
	14	23		A 30
West avenue stone Beltane fires Fifteenth month, 1st to 5th days	15	23	Mayday May 1st	M 31
	16	22		
North avenue stone				J 30
Midsummer sunrise First month	1	23	Solstice June 21st	

Calendar Events Comparison

Year's Eve in our calendar today, so perhaps our festivities had their origins a long time ago.

Mayday and the festivities, the maypole dancing and courting, on 1 May were very popular in Ireland and Britain until the last century. There has been a revival in the west of England in recent years by a group of dedicated enthusiasts. The merrymaking on the ancient anniversary should ensure the continuation of the Beltane festival as the Celtic event was called. On the night, the druids are reputed to have driven their herds of cattle between two bonfires to ensure their health and fertility in the coming year. West avenue stones mark the night five days before 1 May.

The north, east and south avenues mark the nights five days before the Lug, Samain and Imbolc anniversaries. There are a number of very small discrepancies between the ancient anniversary dates and the solar and contemporary dates but the overall pattern is there to be seen, particularly after one takes into account the calendrical shifts that have occurred over the centuries in the Julian and Gregorian calendars.

The four quarter days of 1 May, 1 August, 1 November and 1 February had appreciable legal significance until quite recent times. In Scotland for instance, general legal contracts and tenancy agreements were dated from quarter days, the payment of rent was due on a leased property. Labour contracts were renewed on English farms, and within living memory in northern Holland the farm workers were re-hired for another year on 1 May. How far back these legal practices can be traced is not known; they do however underline the continued importance of the pre-historic dates and customs in everyday life.

Had the strength of folklore and custom been less strong, the advent of the Julian calendar and twelve months could have seen 1 January, 1 March 1 July and 1 September as the quarter days of the year, each being at the start of a three month period. This did not happen however, for custom must have required the continuation of the ancient land tenure practices and the sixteen month quarter days.

Summarising the events of the pre-historic calendar and comparing them with today's Gregorian calendar and the historic records, there appears to be a satis-factory amount of agreement and basic data, the totality of which supports the correctness of the deductions made concerning the basic design and geometry of the Mount Pleasant building. The combination of tradition, folklore memory, the historic Celtic records and the archaeological record attest to the continuation of the ancient traditions for over four and a half thousand years.

Acknowledgements

No book of this kind would be complete without a record of the help and stimulation received from others — my family and friends, the staff of the State Library of Victoria, the Waverley and Nunawading municipal libraries. Particular mention has to be made of the criticism received and aid provided by a number of people, most importantly by Dr Claire O'Kelly and Professor George Eogan.

References have included the following books:

Dr Elizabeth Twohig's, *The Megalithic Art of Western Europe*
C. H. Gordon's, *Forgotten Scripts*
M. Pope's, *The Story of Decipherment*
Martin Brennan's, *The Stars and the Stones*

and a number of other reference books used in the course of my researches. Mention has been made in the general text where particular themes have been discussed.

The author and publisher would like to thank George Eogan and the Office of Public Works for permission to use their photographs.

Bibliography

Atkinson, R. J. C., *Stonehenge*, Penguin, London 1960-79.

Brennan, Martin, *The Stars and the Stones*, Thames and Hudson, London 1983.

Claibone, Robert, *The Birth of Writing*, Time Life, Holland, 1975.

Crossley-Holland, Kevin, *The Norse Myths*, Penguin, London 1982.

Cunliffe, Barry, *The Celtic World*, The Bodley Head, London 1979.

Dillon, Myles, *Irish Sagas*, Mercier Press, Cork, 1968.

Duval, P. M., *Etude Celtiques*, Societe d'Edition Belle Lettres, Paris 1962.

Gordon, C. H., *Forgotten Scripts*, Thames and Hudson, London 1968.

Hubert, H., *The Rise of the Celts*, Kegan Paul, London 1934.

Hubert, H., *The Greatness and Decline of the Celts*, Kegan Paul, London 1934.

McEvedy & Jones, *Atlas of World Population History*, Penguin, London 1978.

O'Neil, W. M., *Time and the Calendars*, Sydney University Press, Sydney 1975.

Pope, Maurice, *The Story of Decipherment*, Thames and Hudson, London 1975.

Rees, Alwyn & Brinley, *Celtic Heritage*, Thames and Hudson, London 1978.

Thomas, Charles, *Britain and Ireland in Early Christian Times*, Thames and Hudson, London 1971.

Thomas, N. L., *British Neolithic Calendar Buildings*, Melbourne, revised edition 1986.

Thomas, N. L. *Stonehenge Sunsets and Thirty-Three*, Melbourne, 1985.

Turville-Petrie, E. O. G., *Myth and Religion in the North*, Weidenfeld & Nicholson, London 1964.

Twohig, E. S., *The Megalithic Art of Western Europe*, Claren-
don Press, Oxford 1981.
Wainwright, C. J., *Mount Pleasant, Dorset, Excavations 1970-71*,
The Society of Antiquaries, London 1979.
The Oxford English Dictionary.
Chambers Encyclopaedia.

Index

Adumla, mythical Norse cow, 89
agriculture, Jordan valley 12, irrigation 12
alignment, mid winter sunrise 50, solar direction 53, symbol 30
alphabet letters 26
arithmetical ability 13
Asgard, Norse gods' domain 90
Ask, first man 90
Australian aboriginies 9

Beltane, Celtic festival 66
Biblical communities 11
Book of Conquests, Irish legends 79
Book of Rights, Irish legends 70
Boyne, the goddess Boand 84, mythological site 81, na Boinne 81, river 18, valley 81
brú, magic dwelling place of the deities 81

Cadbury castle, Arthurian building 83
calendar, British buildings 21, location of buildings 33, comparisons 101, of other civilisations 48, sixteen month 20
Carlyle, Thomas 49
Catal Huyuk, ancient site in Turkey 12
Celtic learning 15, migration 27, society 15
Celts, warlike people 82
Christianity 80, conversion to 82
chronological table of the Irish invasions 87
circles of stones 86
clay tablets 13
climate 13
Conquests, Book of, Irish myth 79
creation myth, Norse 88
Crom Croich 86
Cuculainn 83

Dagda, Irish deity 84
Dark Ages, fifth to seventh centuries AD 15
dawn, alignment 50, mid-winter 51
day symbol 29

Dowth, passage mound 18
diamond symbol 29
direction symbol 30
D'Israeli 25

Egypt 16
Elcmar, Irish deity 84
eleven, symbolic number 76
Eliade, Mircea 79
Embla, first woman 90
England 15
entity symbol 29
equinox 56, alignment 56
Europe, north-west 11

fan design symbol 44
Fir Bolg, Irish prehistoric tribe 80
Fir Domnan, Irish prehistoric tribe 80
firmament, the dome of the sky 89, symbol 30
five day week 35
Fomore, mythical Irish race 80
Fourknocks, prehistoric site in Ireland 75
Fox and Geese, board game 77
Freyrday, day of the week 37

Gallioin, Irish prehistoric tribe 80
Goethe 11
Gregorian calendar 102
group symbol 29

Hallowe'en, Celtic festival 100
hill forts, Celtic defences in England 14
hoop symbol 29

ice age 11,
Iceland 23
Imbolc, Celtic festival 99
invasions, the six of Ireland 79
Ireland 11, invasions 79, settlement 23
Irish calendar 48, myth of the creation 79, symbols 29

Jericho, Palestinian settlement 12

Keasir, Irish prehistoric tribe 80

Knowth passage mound 18, calendar 34, dimensions 36, kerb stone
K 11 56, K 13 38, K 14 41, K 15 43, K 36 59, K 38 60, K 43 60, K 53
61, K 65 63, K 74 57, K 79 67, K 81 69
Knowth passage mound plan 36

Latin the written word 86
learning, method of 15
legend 79
Leinster, Book of 79
line symbol 29
Longfellow 32
Loughcrew, ancient site 22, cairn F 73, cairn X 71
Lug, Celtic deity 85
lunar calendar 61, month 61, symbol 30

mathematical form of calendar 47
May day, Celtic festival 99
megalithic monuments 14,
mesolithic population 11
Middle East lands 12, scripts 31
Midgard, man's domain 90
Mil, Sons of, Irish prehistoric tribe 82
Milesians, Irish prehistoric tribe,= Celts? 82
Minoan inscriptions 28
moon, characteristic behaviour 13, landscape 13, month 61, period
of 29½ days 61, phases 61, symbol 30
Moonday, day of the week 37
Mount Pleasant, prehistoric British site 33, calendar 101, descrip-
tion 98
myths 79
Mythological Cycle, Irish legends 79
mythology 23

Nemed, Irish prehistoric tribe 80
neolithic people of the Isles 11
Newgrange passage mound 17, roof stone 54, stone K 1 50, stone
K 52 53
noon symbol 30
Norse myth of the creation 88
northern latitudes 13
numerical symbols, various 29

Odin, Norse deity 89
Oengus, Irish deity 81, symbol 51

oldest walled city Jericho 12
one symbol 29

papyrus 16
Partholan, Irish prehistoric tribe 80
passage mounds, Dowth 18, Newgrange 17, Knowth 19
Patrick, Saint, the founder of modern Christianity in Ireland 79
population 11
prehistoric man 11

quarters of the year symbol 29

radioactive carbon dates, Newgrange 20, Knowth 20, dating 92
Rees' Alwyn and Brindley 82
Roman Britain 14, Empire 15, invasion of Britain 14
Rosetta stone, Egypt 27
route symbol 30

Samain, Celtic festival 66
Sanctuary, the ancient monument 21
Santorini, climatic effect of the eruption 86
Saxons 15
Scandinavia 15
Scotland 15
script 27
seasons of the year 29, symbol 29
seventeen provinces of Erinn 70, symbolic number 71
Silbury Hill, ancient British monument 14
sixteen month calendar 35
sixteen ray design 44, Knowth K 15 42, Loughcrew X 1 74
Slieve na Calliagh, hills of the witch 71
Snorri Sturlusson, Icelandic chief 88
solar calendar 34
solstice, mid winter 50
spiral symbol 30
stars 24
stone circles 86
Stonehenge, British ancient monument 21
Sumeria 12, writing 13
summer symbol 30
sun characteristic behaviour 13, length of day 13, month 61, symbols 30
Sunday, day of the week 37
symbolic numbers, three — Dowth passage mound 16, Newgrange

passage mound 16, Knowth 16 three mounds: three gods, Odin, Vili and Ve 90, eleven 88, seventeen 70, twenty-two 61, thirty-three 83
symbols Irish 29, other numerical 31

Tartaria writing 28
thirty-three, symbolic number 83, Knowth K 14 41
Thorsday, day of the week 37
Tigernach's Annals, Irish historian 84
Tuatha de Danann, Irish prehistoric tribe 81
twenty-two, symbolic number 61

universe 66
Uruk, Sumerian city 12

Ve, Norse deity 89
vee symbol 29
Viking myth of the creation 88
Vili, Norse deity 89

Wales 15
wavy line symbol 29
White Book of Rhydderch, Welsh legends 76
winter symbol 30
Wodensday, day of the week 37
Woodhenge, ancient British monument 21, design of 21
writing 25

year 64
Ymir, mythical Norse giant 89, skull, the firmament of the sky 89

ziggurat, Middle East building 13
zig-zag symbol 29

A Handbook of Celtic Ornament

J. G. Merne

Apart from its value as a drawing text-book this will be of immense value to all students of arts and crafts – the Merne method for the construction and development of Celtic Ornament has not been surpassed.

An introduction to
IRISH HIGH CROSSES

Hilary Richardson & John Scarry

The Irish high crosses are the most original and interesting of all the monuments which stud the Irish landscape. They are of international importance in early mediaeval art. For their period there is little to equal them in the sculpture of western Europe as a whole.

This beautiful book gives basic information about the crosses. A general survey is followed by an inventory to accompany the large collection of photographs which illustrate their variety and richness. In this way readers will readily have at their disposal an extensive range of the images created in stone by sculptors working in Ireland over a thousand years ago.

The Course of Irish History
Edited by T. W Moody and F. X. Martin

This new revised edition of this excellent book follows the flow of Irish history from the stone age to 1982. The co-operation between historians north and south, Catholic and Protestant makes this book a milestone on the road to national understanding. The twenty-one contributors, all specialists in their own field, use quotations from contemporary writers – chroniclers poets, pamphleteers, government officials – and these quotations, like the fascinating pictures and maps give a touch of life and immediacy too often lacking in works of history.